# ENSEMBLE RICERCARS

RECENT RESEARCHES IN THE MUSIC OF THE RENAISSANCE • VOLUME XXVII

Cristofano Malvezzi
Jacopo Peri
Annibale Padovano

# ENSEMBLE RICERCARS

Edited by Milton A. Swenson

A-R EDITIONS, INC. • MADISON

*To my parents*

ISSN 0486-123X

ISBN 0-89579-089-0

Library of Congress Cataloging in Publication Data:

Main entry under title:

Ensemble ricercars.

   (Recent researches in the music of the Renaissance ;
v. 27 ISSN 0486-123X)
   For 4 unspecified instruments, suitable for viols
(various combinations) or modern bowed string instruments
(various combinations)
   Includes bibliographical references.
   CONTENTS: Malvezzi, C. Terzo tuono.—Malvezzi, C.
Second tuono.—Malvezzi, C. Secondo tuono.—Malvezzi, C.
Primo tuono. [etc.]
   1. Quartets (Unspecified instruments) 2. Chamber
music. I. Malvezzi, Cristofano, 1547-1597. Ricercars,
4-part. c1977. II. Peri, Jacopo, 1561-1633. Ricercars,
4-part. c1977. III. Annibale Padovano, 1527-1575.
Ricercars, 4-part. Selections. c1977. IV. Swenson,
Milton A. V. Series: Recent researches in the music of
the Renaissance; v. 27.
[M486] [M178]  M2.R2384  vol. 27  785.7  77-10848
ISBN 0-89579-089-0

# Contents

# Preface

## The Ensemble Ricercar in the Renaissance Era

The various types of late Renaissance music and their stylistic development have been studied thoroughly with one exception: instrumental ensemble music. Even though sixteenth-century composers were widely involved in writing music for ensemble instruments, the early development of this type of textless music has remained largely unexplored until recent years. Of the many such musical sources that have survived, only a few have been published in modern editions. The present edition contains nine ensemble ricercars by Cristofano Malvezzi, one by Jacopo Peri from Malvezzi's 1577 publication, and five ensemble ricercars by Annibale Padovano originally published in 1566; the edition makes these important works available for modern study and performance. In addition, the following survey of the early development of the ensemble ricercar fills in several gaps in our knowledge of sixteenth-century instrumental music.

The cities of Florence and Venice, where Malvezzi, Peri, and Padovano composed the ricercars contained in this edition, came to be the two most important centers of musical development in the late Renaissance and early baroque. In Venice the musical activities at St. Mark's enjoyed the patronage of the nobility. By the mid-sixteenth century Adriano Willaert, *maestro di cappella* at St. Mark's, had established a tradition of excellence as he incorporated the use of two organs, multiple choirs, and instrumental groups in the grand Venetian style. In Florence, the new generation of Medicis generously supported the arts, lavishing particular interest on the various entertainments (pastoral fables, comedies, processionals) that were so dear to the Florentines. The nobility listened to poetry and music and carried on spirited and partisan discussions in their *academie*.[1] The nature of Greek drama was one of the topics often debated in these intellectual discussions. These discussions would eventually produce the first opera and a revolution in music.

Although ricercars for lute and for keyboard instruments had been composed earlier, the first appearance of ensemble ricercars (those published in partbooks) was in a publication entitled *Musica Nova*, printed in Venice in 1540,[2] and containing music by Adriano Willaert and other composers (Giulio Segni, Girolamo Parabosco, Girolamo Cavazzoni, Nicolo Benoist, and Guilielmo Colin) closely associated with the Venetian School under Willaert's leadership.

The importance of the works in *Musica Nova* lies in their adaptation of the imitative techniques of the motet to an extended instrumental composition, thus establishing the imitative ensemble ricercar. In this adaptation, however, the ensemble ricercar goes far beyond the concept of a textless motet; there are numerous repetitions of thematic material and frequent use of the learned contrapuntal devices of augmentation, diminution, inversion, and retrograde. The structure of these ricercars is unified by simultaneously combining statements of two or more different themes or by modifying one theme to form another one. Contrast is often achieved by introducing a passage in triple meter within the overall duple mensuration or by using shorter note values to quicken the harmonic rhythm. Other style characteristics employed by the *Musica Nova* composers include the use of the *La-Sol-Fa-Re-Mi* solmization theme (Willaert), the repetition of brief sections (Segni, Colin), the use of a Gregorian chant melody as a *cantus firmus* (Parabosco), and parody (Segni). Unlike the earlier improvisatory lute and keyboard ricercars, the masterfully organized structural and contrapuntal fitting-together of themes evidenced in the *Musica Nova* ricercars eliminates the possibility of their being called improvisatory works. In fact, this carefully worked out structure and style is the "new" element referred to in the title, *Musica Nova;* this compositional technique represents the beginning of a new art form.

The "new music" ricercar style was disseminated mainly through the Venetian associates and students (Jacques Buus, Antonio Barges, Annibale Padovano, Andrea Gabrieli, and Claudio Merulo) of the master teacher Adriano Willaert. Ensemble ricercar composers outside this Venetian circle include Giuliano Tiburtino (Tivoli) and Giovanni Battista Conforti (Parma?).

Buus' eighteen four-part ensemble ricercars, published in 1547 and 1549,[3] continued the tradition of the *Musica Nova* composers in the numerous theme repetitions and use of the learned contrapuntal devices; however, the most obvious characteristic of these ricercars is their extended length. Buus is also known as the composer of the earliest monothematic ricercar (Recercar quatro [sic] from Book I).

The little-known composer Giovanni Battista Conforti, who seems to have had no connection with Willaert's Venetian School, included fourteen four-part ensemble ricercars in a publication of 1558, *Il Primo Libro de Ricercari*.[4] In these pieces Conforti used many of the style characteristics previously found in music by the *Musica Nova* composers. These include mosaic-like contrapuntal structure resulting from the simultaneous entries of two or more themes, use of the *La-Sol-Fa-Re-Mi* solmization theme, monothematic ricercars (two examples), thematic modification, and frequent use of the learned contrapuntal devices, particularly augmentation. Perhaps Conforti's most important contributions to the development of the ensemble ricercar are his creative treatment of harmony and modulation and his development of contrasts in harmonic and rhythmic movement. Consonant harmonic passages are skillfully juxtaposed with modulatory passages or dissonant harmony that includes accented passing tones and chains of suspensions; sections employing a slow, static harmonic and rhythmic movement are alternated with passages in fast harmonic rhythm with small note-values, short motivic themes, syncopations, and dance-like rhythms. The artful and effective use of these elements of contrast contributes to the aesthetic interest of Conforti's ricercars.

Andrea Gabrieli's ensemble ricercars are well known to modern scholars. One of these works, written for eight voices and published in 1587, is similar in style to the ensemble canzonas for two antiphonal choirs composed by his nephew, Giovanni Gabrieli.[5] Andrea's remaining seven ensemble ricercars are four-part works, published in 1589.[6] Although these ricercars first appeared in published form after Andrea's death in 1586, analysis and comparison of the works suggest that they were composed at an earlier date than Malvezzi's 1577 works.[7] Five of Gabrieli's four-part ricercars (I, II, III, IV, and VI of the 1589 publication) conform to the "normal" pattern of the imitative ricercar. These works continue the tradition of exhaustive repetition of themes and the use of the learned contrapuntal devices. Similar to one of Willaert's works (Ricercar X, *Musica Nova*, 1540), these ricercars use the duplex theme[8] where the opening theme consists of two sections separated by a rest (A$_{1-2}$), with the entries of A$_2$

forming a counter-subject to the entries of A$_1$. Gabrieli employs this two-part theme in a highly organized way with each section of the theme being developed separately, in combination with one another, or in simultaneous combination with other themes. Gabrieli's remaining four-part ricercars (Ricercars V and VII of the 1589 publication) are remarkably different from the others. Their style is characterized by the use of repeated-note themes, stretto, motivic imitation, familiar style, motivic themes, and the repetition of lengthy sections; in fact, these two ricercars have been labeled canzonas by some scholars although their canzona-like aspects may also be found in ricercars by Conforti, Segni, Colin, Parabosco, and Willaert. Additional aspects of Andrea Gabrieli's style include sparing use of dissonance (this contributes to their static harmonic style) and use of new modes (namely, Ricercar VI "del Nono Tuono" and Ricercar VII "del Duodecimo Tuono") based on Glarean's system of twelve modes.[9]

Although Claudio Merulo is best known for his organ works, he made significant contributions to the development of the ensemble ricercar. Not only did he write more ensemble ricercars than any other composer (there are sixty four-part works), but he also used new stylistic devices that were important steps in the development of the baroque fugue. Merulo's ricercars appeared in three publications, each being printed as a set of four partbooks: Book I (1574, nineteen ricercars), Book II (1607, twenty-one ricercars), and Book III (1608, twenty ricercars). The latter two books were published posthumously.[10] A full set of four partbooks, however, is extant only for the 1574 publication. None of these works has appeared in a modern edition although a few of them have recently been transcribed.[11] In many respects Merulo's ensemble pieces represent simply a continuation of the Venetian ricercar tradition. The themes, usually vocal in style, are treated contrapuntally. Frequently, several themes are combined simultaneously, resulting in the mosaic-like contrapuntal structure used by Willaert and others. At least one of Merulo's ricercars is monothematic; he also used the duplex theme. Merulo's conservative harmony is another characteristic that marks him as a composer of the Venetian School. With the exception of inversion, Merulo used the learned contrapuntal devices rarely. An innovative method of using inversion occurs in several of his ricercars where statements of the opening theme are answered by this same theme in its inverted form. This contrapuntal technique later came to be called a "counter-fugue" or "inverted fugue."[12] Another bold innovation (also involving the contrapuntal treatment of themes) encountered in Merulo's ricercars of 1574 is the earliest appearance of the technique which later came to be called "double fugue." There are two double-fugue ricercars in Merulo's Book I collection and there is even an example of a "quadruple fugue." These contrapuntal innovations were important in the development of the fugue to the time of J. S. Bach.

Annibale Padovano's ensemble ricercars were published in 1556; by that time the Venetian innovation of an extended imitative work without text had already become well established. Malvezzi's *Il Primo Libro de Ricercari* was published in 1577. As has been shown, during the twenty-one years between Padovano's and Malvezzi's publications, several other composers contributed new ideas to the development of the ensemble ricercar. Style characteristics of the compositions in Padovano's and Malvezzi's publications will be discussed below.

## The Composers

### Malvezzi

Cristofano Malvezzi was one of the revolutionary composers of the late Renaissance who helped to usher in the baroque age. He was born June 28, 1547,[13] in the city of Lucca, not far from Florence. His father, Nicolao Malvezzi, was organist at the cathedral of San Martino in Lucca.[14] Cristofano received his early musical training from his father until 1557 when Nicolao died. It is likely that he is the same "Christolo della malvasia" who was associated with Jaches Brumel at the court of the Duke of Ferrara in 1558.[15] Later, Cristofano may have continued his musical education in Florence with Francesco Corteccia, *maestro di cappella* to Cosimo I dei Medici.[16] The death of Donato Valdambrini created a vacancy in the post of canon at the church of San Lorenzo which Malvezzi was appointed to fill; Malvezzi retained this sinecure from about 1572 until his death.[17] Sometime before 1577 (the year in which his ricercars of the present edition were published) Malvezzi had succeeded Corteccia in the post of *maestro di cappella* to the Medici choir.[18] Malvezzi served in this prestigious position until his death on Christmas Day in 1597. His grave is at the church of San Lorenzo.

Malvezzi was deeply involved in the exciting musical developments taking place in Florence. Not only did he collaborate with Giulio Caccini, Emilio dei Cavalieri, and Luca Marenzio in setting to music the intermezzi for various comedies presented in Florence (the librettists for which included Count Giovanni Bardi and Ottavo Rinuccini)[19] but he was also the teacher of Jacopo Peri. According to D. P. Walker, it is likely that Malvezzi was a member of the Florentine *Camerata*.[20]

Besides his dramatic music, some of which was published in the *Intermedii e Concerti* of 1591 (composed for the wedding of Ferdinando dei Medici and Cristina di Lorraine),[21] Malvezzi's extant works include two books of madrigals à 5 (1583 and 1590), one book of madrigals à 6 (1584), several madrigals in published anthologies,[22] three pieces for vocal solo and basso continuo arranged from part songs,[23] an instrumental canzona surviving in the organ tablature book of the German colorist Bernhard Schmid the younger,[24] and the four-part ensemble ricercars of 1577.

### Peri

Jacopo Peri ("il Zazzerino") was born on August 20, 1561. Although it is likely that Jacopo was born in Rome, he spent most of his lifetime in Florence where his father was a nobleman.[25] Malvezzi was Peri's first teacher of counterpoint, and by 1577 Peri had become accomplished enough to compose a ricercar worthy of inclusion in his teacher's publication. During this time Malvezzi also may have instructed Peri in playing keyboard instruments and possibly even in the art of singing. By 1577 Peri had already acquired the nickname "il Zazzerino," given him for his beautiful long auburn hair.[26] A letter written by Cavalieri dated November 10, 1600, affirms that Peri was still known by this nickname: "He [Rinuccini] says that what difficulties this style [the new *stile rappresentativo*] presented were surmounted by the great science in music possessed by Jacopo Peri, that is il Zazzerino."[27]

Another letter written in 1634[28] emphasizes Peri's skills as a keyboard performer and composer of counterpoint:

> Also in Florence at this time was Jacopo Peri, who, as the first pupil of Cristofano Malvezzi, received high praise as a player of the organ and the keyboard instruments and as a composer of counterpoint and was highly regarded as second to none of the singers of that city.

Although Peri's reputation as a fine singer is generally recognized and his life and works from about 1595 are well known, the fact that he was also known as a composer of counterpoint and as a performer on keyboard instruments has been overshadowed by his later operatic accomplishments.

By about 1580 Peri was a member of the *Camerata* under its first patron and leader, Count Bardi. After Bardi left for Rome in 1592, Peri continued his association with this group of musical revolutionaries now under the leadership of Jacopo Corsi. In 1583 a madrigal by Peri was included in a publication of five-part madrigals by Malvezzi, and the following year the young composer and singer was invited to perform for the duke and duchess of Mantua.[29]

Dramatic compositions by Peri include the fifth intermezzo to Bargagli's comedy *La Pellegrina* (composed in 1589 for the wedding of Ferdinando I dei Medici and Cristina di Lorraine), the opera *Dafne* (Peri seems to have started this as early as 1594),[30] *Euridice* (1600), the recitatives of the opera *Arianna* (the arias were composed by Monteverdi),[31] and much incidental music for the many Florentine festival presentations.

In addition to this dramatic music, Peri composed madrigals, several of which are in monodic style. His only known instrumental work (No. [9], p. 36 of the present edition) is contained in Malvezzi's collection of ricercars, published in 1577. By 1618 Peri had retired from singing, and his last known composition comes from the year 1625. He died in 1633 at the age of seventy-two, a victim of a severe epidemic which swept Florence. He is buried in the church of S. Maria Novella.[32]

*Padovano*

Annibale Padovano was born in Padua in the year 1527. On November 30, 1553, when Padovano was twenty-six, the procurators of St. Mark's cathedral in Venice appointed him organist to fill the position left by the aging Frate Giovanni Armonio.[33] Padovano remained at St. Mark's until 1563.[34] Adriano Willaert was *maestro di cappella* there from 1527 until his death in 1562. During this time the music at the private chapel of the Doges reached its greatest splendor. St. Mark's had the distinction of having two separate organs, one on either side of the church. Padovano played one of these organs, while the appointment to the other was held successively by Girolamo Parabosco (1551-1557) and Claudio Merulo (1557-1584).[35] Padovano and Parabosco initiated the practice of playing both organs together for processionals on high feast days.[36] This had important consequences for the Venetian style of the early baroque. Also, it is known that Padovano and Merulo played in other churches besides St. Mark's.[37] Other Venetian associates of Padovano were Cipriano de Rore, Andrea Gabrieli, and Gioseffo Zarlino.

It is not known exactly when Padovano left St. Mark's. Although he did not submit his final resignation until 1566, he had already been called to Graz in 1565 to serve as court organist to the Austrian Archduke Charles II.[38] Charles had become Archduke on the death of Emperor Ferdinand in 1564. As he organized the court chapel at Graz, Charles appointed a singer from Vienna, Johannes de Cleve, as the first *Kapellmeister* in 1564; Padovano's appointment as court organist with the title "obrister Musicus" (supreme musician) followed a year later.[39] Even though the court organist had the duty of playing for chapel services, Padovano was not a member of the court chapel; instead, he and the other court instrumentalists were under the management of the royal stables.[40] In 1568 Padovano composed and directed works for multiple choirs for the wedding celebration of Duke Wilhelm V of Bavaria in Munich.[41] When de Cleve resigned his position as *Kapellmeister* in 1570 "for reasons of health," Padovano was appointed to take his place.[42] Five years later at the end of March 1575, Padovano died in Graz at the age of forty-nine.

Padovano's fame is demonstrated by the fact that his works were frequently published and copied more than twenty-five years after his death, and also by the high esteem his contemporaries accorded him. In a letter written to Archduke Charles II in 1565 by the Imperial ambassador to Venice, Franz von Thurn, Padovano and Cipriano de Rore were praised as the two "perhaps most famous Italian men."[43] The Archduchess Maria, who was one of Padovano's students, wrote a letter to her brother in which she mourned Padovano's death, writing that "it is the end of my training in his art; there will be a skip in my heartbeat."[44] Finally, Vincenzo Galilei in his *Dialogo della musica antica e della moderna* of 1581 praised Padovano as having been an excellent player and composer of keyboard music.[45]

Although Annibale Padovano is often recognized primarily as a composer of organ music, he is represented by a considerable number of works of other types. His vocal music includes books of madrigals, motets, and Masses; most of the vocal works were composed after he left Venice. His eight-part motets and his Mass for twenty-four voice parts show that he continued the Venetian experiments of writing music for a large number of voices. His extant keyboard music is limited to three toccatas and two ricercars for organ that were published posthumously in 1604.[46] His ensemble music includes a late work for eight instruments, *Aria della Battaglia per Sonar à 8*;[47] "twelve-voice 'concerti' scored for six viols, one zink [cornetto], five trombones, and a regal";[48] and the thirteen ensemble ricercars published in 1556, his earliest-known works.

## The Music

Although Malvezzi's, Peri's, and Padovano's works continue in the tradition of the imitative four-part ensemble ricercar, there are also some aspects of their music that are characteristic of the transition from the Renaissance to the baroque. Use of two or more themes, rhythmic transformation of themes, repeated-note themes, division of the music into sections, and specific designation of modes are characteristics that exist in music of all three composers. These elements and the more specialized aspects found in the ricercars in the present edition are discussed below.[49]

Each composer used more than one theme in his ricercars. The number of themes used in Malvezzi's music ranges from two (Ricercar [10]) to seven (Ricercar [1]). There are eight themes in Peri's Ricercar [9]. Padovano's music generally has a large number of themes; there are eight themes in Ricercar [14], thirteen in Ricercar [12], and seventeen in Ricercar [11].

Modification of one theme to form another theme (see Example 1) occurs in all of Malvezzi's pieces with the exception of Ricercars [6] and [10]. Padovano also made frequent use of this technique (Example 1). However, both in Padovano's *Ricercar del Terzo Tono* [13] and in Peri's Ricercar [9] all themes are independently conceived; there is no thematic modification to form new themes.

Malvezzi and Peri also varied their themes by means of rhythmic transformation. In Example 2, the several statements of Theme A in Malvezzi's Ricercar [2] retain exactly the same melodic contour while changing the rhythmic values of some of the notes.[50]

Ex. 2. Malvezzi, Ricercar [2].

Although they resemble augmentation or diminution at times, these rhythmic alterations are basically free.

Repeated-note themes are used by all three composers. A good example of a repeated-note theme occurs in Malvezzi's Ricercar [7] where the A-theme begins with the repeated-note figure ♩ ♩ ♩ often associated with the canzona.

Although the form of ricercars is often described simply as through-composed, a careful analysis of the works in the present edition will almost always reveal division of the pieces into sections by means of changes in thematic or contrapuntal treatment, changes of meter, conclusive cadences, or some combination of these.

All three composers designated the specific mode for each of their ricercars. However, differences exist in each composer's modal treatment. This treatment and other specific aspects of compositional technique are discussed in the material on each composer that follows.

*Malvezzi's Style*

Malvezzi used a variety of thematic material in addition to the repeated-note technique mentioned above. The solmization theme *La-Sol-Fa-Re-Mi* appears in Ricercar [4], theme B (see Example 3), and has seventy-five entries. A chromatic theme moving by half-steps occurs in Ricercar [6]

Ex. 1a. Malvezzi, Ricercar [1].

Theme A (m. 1 ff.)

Theme A'1 (m. 19 ff.)

Theme A'2 (m. 27 ff.)

Theme A'3 (m. 64 ff.)

Ex. 1b. Padovano, Ricercar [11].

Theme A, *Kyrie Cunctipotens Genitor* (m. 1 ff.)

A' 3  A' 4  A' 2  A' 1

Theme A'1 (m. 12 ff.)

Theme A'2 (m. 13 ff.)

Theme A'3 (m. 35 ff.)

Theme A'4 (m. 57 ff.)

(mm. 40 ff.) not only in its original ascending progression, but also in its inverted form (mm. 46 ff.). This use of chromaticism is a style characteristic not seen before in the ensemble ricercar; it was used later by the early baroque composers Frescobaldi and Sweelinck. Opening themes in Malvezzi's ricercars are often lengthy (three to four measures), while subsequent themes are short and motivic. Example 1 illustrates this contrast. These motivic themes along with disjunct melodic lines (wide leaps, crossing of voice parts, and wide voice ranges) give Malvezzi's ricercars an instrumental character not found in the music of Peri or Padovano. Frequent thematic repetition is another common feature of Malvezzi's style. The repetition of the solmization theme has already been discussed; and although none of Malvezzi's other themes has such a great number of repetitions, theme C of Ricercar [5] (mm. 38 ff., 75 ff.) enters forty-one times, theme A of Ricercar [7] has thirty-five statements, and two other themes (theme A'2 of Ricercar [2] and theme D of Ricercar [3]) have as many as thirty-two entries.

The contrapuntal texture of Malvezzi's ricercars is a significant aspect of his style. Much of Malvezzi's music has a mosaic-like contrapuntal texture; different themes are stated simultaneously in each of the four voice parts. Examples of this kind of counterpoint exist in Ricercars [4] and [8].

The counterpoint of Malvezzi's opening expositions is often innovative. In Ricercar [5], for example, the Altus voice part remains *tacet* until measure 24, where the A-theme enters, producing an opening exposition that is longer than the opening exposition of any ensemble ricercar previously written. There is a spaciousness in this ricercar caused not only by the extended length of theme A, but also by Malvezzi's use of a codetta between the second and third entries of the theme; this eight-measure codetta includes new thematic material (theme B), motivic imitation, and a diminution of theme A.

Malvezzi also used the "double-fugue" type of ricercar (see Ricercar [4], Example 3) initiated by Merulo three years earlier.

In Ricercar [4], theme A is combined with the *La-Sol-Fa-Re-Mi* theme (theme B) for the first two entries (mm. 1-2, Altus and Tenor) as is shown in Example 3. This is followed by a short two-voice codetta with diminution of theme B (m. 4) before the Cantus and Bass parts enter with a second combination of themes A and B. Theme A of this piece is also derived from the *La-Sol-Fa-Re-Mi* solmization pattern, but at the third note of this theme (see Example 3), there is a shift from one hexachord to another.[51]

Malvezzi used Merulo's "counterfugue" technique, as well. Although counterfugues exist in his Ricercars [1], [6], [7], and [8], Malvezzi's organization of opening expositions is not nearly as strict as Merulo's. In Ricercar [1], for instance, theme A and its inversion are combined simultaneously in the first two entries (Cantus and Tenor); however, for the third and fourth entries (Altus and Bass, mm. 9 and 10 respectively) the inversion, only, is employed. The combination of theme A with its inversion occurs only once throughout the work. Theme A, with only three statements in the entire piece, has no exposition; instead, this theme serves as a source from which the three modifications illustrated in Example 1 and the inversion are generated. Ricercars [7] and [8] have similar loosely-organized opening expositions. Malvezzi used the counterfugue technique differently in the opening exposition of Ricercar [6], however. Here, the first two voice parts enter with statements of theme A and the third and fourth voices follow with statements of its inversion. Although theme A is not actually combined with its inversion in the opening exposition, this combination does occur later in the piece at measures 18, 29, and 87.

Another of Malvezzi's irregular opening expositions, although not of the counterfugue type, occurs in Ricercar [3]. Here, the opening entries of theme A are stated in the Altus and Cantus voice parts, after which a new theme is used for the initial entries of the Bass (theme B) and Tenor parts (theme B augmented). Even the statements of the A-theme are irregular in this piece. There are two versions of theme A (see Example 4).

Ex. 3. Malvezzi, Ricercar [4], mm. 1-5

Ex. 4. Malvezzi, Ricercar [3], mm. 1-4

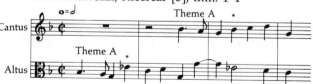

The first version (Altus part) has the interval of a minor sixth between notes 3 and 4; this interval is a minor third in the second version (Cantus part). The first version of theme A occurs only twice (m. 1 and m. 23) throughout the entire work; the remaining nine entries of theme A use the second version.

Except for Ricercar [10], the learned contrapuntal devices are found in all of Malvezzi's ricercars. Inversion is used much more frequently than any of the other devices. Malvezzi had several methods of treating the inverted themes. One of these, the counterfugue technique, is described above. Counterfugue technique occurs frequently in opening expositions, and occasionally later on in the ricercars (e.g., Ricercar [1], theme D and its inversion, m. 76 ff.; Ricercar [8], theme A and its inversion, m. 46 ff.). Another treatment of inverted themes is to develop them in a regular four-voice exposition (see the inverted solmization theme B of Ricercar [4], m. 29 ff.). Still another procedure is the use of an inverted theme as accompaniment to either an augmentation of that theme or to an entirely different theme. For instance, in Ricercar [2] (mm. 19-24) the inversion of one of the modifications of theme A accompanies, in the three upper voices, a four-fold augmentation of theme A in the Bass. This same procedure is repeated immediately thereafter (mm. 29-35), but the augmentation is in the Cantus part (beginning in m. 27).

Although diminution in Malvezzi's ricercars is rare, augmentation occurs frequently. The augmented theme is never presented in an organized exposition; instead, the augmentation is usually combined with another theme or themes to form a dense contrapuntal texture. There is a truly innovative instance of augmentation in Ricercar [4] where the solmization theme B is expanded to four times its original value, being at the same time broken apart by the insertion of a breve rest between each of its notes (m. 83 ff.).

The elements of stretto and motivic imitation give Malvezzi's music a "nervous" quality. Malvezzi used stretto frequently in all of his works; good examples of stretto are found in Ricercar [3] (theme C, m. 37 ff.) and in Ricercar [5] (theme C, m. 86 ff.). Motivic imitation occurs occasionally, also; examples may be seen in the spacious opening exposition of Ricercar [5], in measures 28-31 of Ricercar [1], and in measures 75-77 of Ricercar [3].

There are short canonic passages in three of Malvezzi's pieces. In Ricercar [10] canons are used both in a codetta as an extension of theme A (mm. 2-8) and, later, as short episodes between thematic expositions (mm. 23-26, 36-37). Two canons in Ricercar [8] (mm. 30-32, 65-68) are also used as episodic material. A canonic passage serves a different purpose in Ricercar [4] (mm. 52-56) where the canon, located in the Bass and Cantus parts, accompanies statements of theme B, forming a mosaic-like contrapuntal structure.

Contrapuntally, Ricercar [10] differs from Malvezzi's other pieces in that: (1) its two themes are exposed and developed in two completely separate sections without the use of simultaneous combination of themes; (2) it is the only work in which Malvezzi uses a tonal answer in an exposition; and (3) none of the learned contrapuntal devices is used. There is also a complete lack of mosaic-like counterpoint in this ricercar.

Malvezzi's ricercars are usually divided into sections by cadences that are quite conclusive although a few sections close with inconclusive deceptive cadences. The number of sections in the ricercars ranges from four (Ricercar [10]) to seven (Ricercars [7] and [8]). For example, Ricercar [8] is divided into seven sections at measures 9, 17, 33, 40, 50, and 70. Each section has a distinctive contrapuntal treatment, and each (except for the sectional division at m. 50) ends with a conclusive cadence. Although there is no definitive cadence at measure 50, a sectional division seems indicated by the beginning of the fourfold augmentation of theme A. The closing section, beginning at measure 70, is marked by a change from duple to triple meter that achieves a heightened contrast at the end of the piece.

Malvezzi used Glarean's system of twelve modes to identify the tonality of the ricercars in his collection; he designated the mode of each piece in its title. Several of the works follow the practice of transposing the tonality up a fourth by the use of a b-flat key signature. Two of these pieces, Ricercar [8] "del Undecimo Tuono" and Ricercar [6] "senza unisoni del Duodecimo Tuono"—in modes XI and XII respectively, and normally with their finals on c, forming the "C-major" scale—are transposed to the "F-major" scale by means of their b-flat key signatures and finals on f. In fact, Malvezzi would not have had to follow this procedure in composing these two ricercars in the "F-major" scale; instead, he could have labeled them as modes V and VI, using the b-flat key signature and finals on f. This latter method of using what was later to be called the "F-major" scale had been common practice in the time of Josquin des Pres[52] and was also encountered in Padovano's ensemble ricercars.

Other modal peculiarities occur in Malvezzi's Ricercar [4] "del Primo Tuono," which has the normal final on d. This piece is remarkable in that the final tonality is avoided for all but one of its intermediate cadences. Instead, the intermediate cadences occur most frequently on c, followed by e, a, and g. In Ricercar [7] "del Settimo Tuono," the final cadence, which is on g, sounds more like a half-cadence in the tonality of c than like a final plagal cadence in the seventh mode. This tonal ambiguity is caused by the two conclusive cadences on c occurring in measures 101 and 102 and by the emphasis on c tonality in the measures immediately preceding these cadences.

Malvezzi's harmony, particularly his chromaticism, is probably the most important aspect of his style. In Ricercar [6] (mm. 42-51) there is the exposition of the four-note chromatic theme combined with its inversion which was described above. Such chromaticism may have been an expression of humanistic interest in Greek musical theory. Another example of Malvezzi's progressive chromatic style occurs in Ricercar [7] (mm. 72-77) where c-sharp, f-sharp, and g-sharp are used with great frequency in close proximity. Such experiments are remarkable since they occurred before the chromaticism of Frescobaldi, Gesualdo, and Giovanni da Macque.

Parallel fifths and octaves were used frequently by Malvezzi; in every case, however, the parallelism is visually concealed by a crossing or exchange of voice parts. One noteworthy example is in Ricercar [8] (mm. 75-76), where hidden parallel fifths and octaves occur simultaneously, followed immediately by another set of parallel fifths in the next measure.

Malvezzi used short modulatory passages quite often as a means of adding diversity to the harmonic texture. For instance, in measures 53-55 of Ricercar [2] the tonality, beginning in "F major," modulates first to "D minor," and then to "C major." Other modulatory passages are found in Ricercar [2] (mm. 65-66, 92) and in Ricercar [10] (m. 21). Also contributing to the variety of harmonic style are Malvezzi's frequent passages where the melody of one voice part moves in syncopation with the other three voices, producing a syncopated harmonic movement as well as a quickening of the harmonic rhythm. Short passages illustrating this technique occur in Ricercar [2] (mm. 45-46 and 91), in Ricercar [3] (mm. 48-49), and in Ricercar [5] (mm. 45-47, 66-70, and 84-94).

There are still other extraordinary elements in Malvezzi's harmonic style. Malvezzi's Ricercar [6] has in its title the unusual designation "senza unisoni" (without unisons), indicating that there is an absence of vertical unisons throughout the piece. The cadence at measures 22-23 of Ricercar [6] exhibits an irregular voice-leading into the chord of resolution. Each voice part exchanges its normal note of resolution with that of another voice part. Two other unusual cadences occurring at the end of Ricercar [6] (mm. 84-85, 89-90) make effective use of the $V^7$ chord. A further example of Malvezzi's remarkable harmonic practice is the double leading-tone cadence in Ricercar [7] (mm. 94-95).

Finally, there are a number of interesting dissonant passages in Malvezzi's works. Cross relations occur in Ricercar [2] (m. 48) where an e-flat in the Bass is juxtaposed with an e-natural in the Cantus, in Ricercar [6] (mm. 14-15) where a b-flat and a b-natural are notated side by side in the Bass and Cantus, and in Ricercar [4] (m. 59) where the dissonance of f-natural against f-sharp is emphasized by the absence of octave separation and by the suspension dissonance (g against f) that occurs on the third beat of the measure. Another harsh dissonance occurs in Ricercar [2] (m. 86) where the adjacent pitches f, g, and a appear simultaneously and without octave separation on the last beat of the measure. This dissonance was intended by Malvezzi; it could not have resulted from scribal error since the dissonant tone g is part of the theme.

## Peri's Style

In Ricercar [9] Peri did not repeat his themes nearly as often as Malvezzi did. Both opening and subsequent themes are rarely more than two measures in length. Peri's melodies have a narrow range and are predominantly conjunct; the melodic material is more vocally oriented than Malvezzi's.

Although Peri's contrapuntal treatment is not as complex as Malvezzi's, it confirms the fact that Peri was more than the amateur he has so often been pictured; indeed, he was a musician in the fullest sense of the word. The most salient feature of Peri's style is the transparency and elegance of his counterpoint. Although theme A is used in combination with most of the other seven themes of Ricercar [9], the texture of his thematic combinations is not as thick as Malvezzi's. Inversion and augmentation are found to a limited extent in Peri's ricercar. Diminution occurs more frequently; there is a three-voice exposition of the diminution of theme A (mm. 39 ff.) that accelerates the contrapuntal and harmonic movement. Another aspect that also tends to animate the contrapuntal movement is Peri's use of stretto; stretto occurs frequently with themes C (mm. 19 ff.), D (mm. 25-30), and E (mm. 33 ff.). Example 5 illustrates Peri's use of stretto with theme D where three sets of paired-stretto entries are juxtaposed.

Ex. 5. Peri, Ricercar [9]
(theme D, paired-stretto entries)

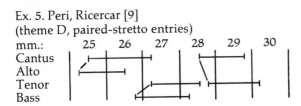

A progressive aspect of Peri's style that foreshadows the baroque fugue is the consistent use of the tonal answer for every exposition of theme A where the opening leap of a perfect fifth in the thematic statements is displaced in the answers by the leap of a perfect fourth. It is also interesting to note that Ricercar [9] is completely polyphonic; there is no trace of the homophonic texture that was later to become such an important aspect of Peri's style. In fact, his use of the old points-of-imitation polyphonic structure plus the absence of definitive intermediate cadences makes it difficult to locate sectional divisions in Peri's ricercar.

The harmonic style of Ricercar [9] is elegant and polished. There is not nearly as much chromaticism as in Malvezzi's ricercars, nor does Peri use syncopated harmonic movement. However, in two effective passages (mm. 34-36 and mm. 39-40) Peri briefly speeds up the harmonic rhythm to provide contrast. The second of these passages (mm. 39-40) also contains the stretto exposition of theme A in diminution mentioned above.

## Padovano's Style

Padovano frequently used Gregorian melodies as themes for his ricercars. In Padovano's Ricercar [11] "del Primo Tono" the A-theme (see Example 1) is derived from the Gregorian chant melody *Kyrie Cunctipotens Genitor*.[53] Not only did Padovano announce this melody in an exposition at the beginning of the piece and use it as a generator of new themes, but he also used it as a *cantus firmus* in long note values (longas, dotted longas, and even a double longa). The first half of the melody is stated as a *cantus firmus* in the Tenor (mm. 14-30). Then, a single statement of the last half of the melody, beginning with the *eleison* section, is presented as a migrating *cantus firmus* (see Exam-

ple 6) that starts in the Tenor (mm. 32-40) and moves, successively, to the Bass (mm. 41-43), the Cantus (mm. 44-46), the Altus (mm. 47-49), the Cantus (mm. 50-52), and back to the Tenor (mm. 53-55).[54]

Ex. 6. Padovano, Ricercar [11]: Migrating *cantus firmus* treatment of the *Kyrie Cunctipotens Genitor* melody (second half).

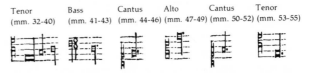

This treatment of the *cantus firmus* melody could be viewed as a sixteenth-century instance of musical pointillism comparable to Anton Webern's *Klangfarbenmelodie*-setting of Johann Sebastian Bach's ricercar from *The Musical Offering*.

Padovano's use of Gregorian melodies is not confined to Ricercar [11]. His Ricercar [13] "del Terzo Tono" has the melody *Pange lingua gloriosi* as its second theme (m. 32 ff.),[55] and Ricercar [15] "del Primo Tono" is based on the first psalm tone, D-termination (mm. 38-50).[56] Padovano's Ricercar [14] "del Quinto Tono" employs both the antiphon *Qui pacem ponit* (mm. 1-38) and the termination of the fifth psalm tone (mm. 83-110);[57] the fifth psalm tone is used in a thematic exposition by itself, including stretto entries (mm. 83-95) that are followed by a slightly altered version of this theme combined with another theme (mm. 96-101). In the broadly climactic closing section of Ricercar [14] the altered version of the theme is augmented four times its original value and used as a *cantus firmus* in the highest voice part (mm. 106-110). Padovano was not the first composer to use Gregorian melodies in ricercars. Girolamo Parabosco, who was Padovano's associate at St. Mark's when these works were published, composed an ensemble ricercar based on the Gregorian chant melody *Da Pacem* that had been published in *Musica Nova* (1540). There is also a non-liturgical concordant melody in Padovano's Ricercar [12] whose initial theme bears a strong similarity to the beginning of Fiorenzo Maschera's *Canzona detta la Villarchiaro*.[58]

With the exception of Ricercar [11], Padovano's themes are less than three measures long; there is little difference in length between opening and subsequent themes. Padovano's themes average between ten and twelve repetitions throughout his ricercars, although many of them have a much larger number of entries. For example, theme A'4 of Ricercar [11] has a total of thirty-six entries.

The melodic movement of these themes is conjunct and vocally oriented.

The counterpoint in Padovano's ricercars includes both conservative and progressive elements. In many of his ricercars Padovano used the old motet style of points-of-imitation where each theme is exposed in turn without use of unifying devices of any kind. This points-of-imitation technique occurs most frequently in Ricercars [12] and [13]. Ricercars [11] and [14] are more progressive in that they contain the unifying devices of simultaneous combination of different themes, modification of one theme to form another, and the return of previously exposed themes, resulting in a mosaic-like structure.

Spacious opening expositions are a hallmark of Padovano's style.[59] For instance, in Ricercar [11] the fourth voice part does not make its initial entry with theme A until measure 14. The spaciousness here is not caused so much by the length of the theme as by Padovano's use of two codettas, one between the second and third entries, the other between the third and fourth. Long opening expositions are also found in several other of his ricercars.[60]

Most of the learned contrapuntal devices were used frequently by Padovano. Augmentation is most often found in conjunction with liturgical themes as a means of producing a final climax. A remarkable example of this occurs at the end of Ricercar [15] (mm. 114-124) where the fifth-tone termination melody is presented as a two-part canon augmented four times its original value. Although it is not strictly used, inversion is occasionally found; an example is Ricercar [14] (mm. 37-39) where only the first three notes of the inverted A-theme follow the original version exactly. Stretto occurs in Ricercar [12] with theme F (mm. 138-149) and in Ricercar [11] with theme E (mm. 88-90).[61]

The number of sections in Padovano's works ranges from six (Ricercar [14]) to fourteen (Ricercar [12]). Sectional divisions in Padovano's ricercars are often difficult to ascertain. This is particularly true of Ricercars [12] and [13] where the old motet style of a series of points-of-imitation is used; the formal structure of these ricercars is outlined by the beginnings and endings of the points with few definitive intermediate cadences.[62] Padovano's Ricercar [14], on the other hand, has sections that are clearly outlined by conclusive cadences. This piece is divided into six sections at measures 43, 61, 83, 97, and 111. The final section of Ricercar [14] is a short cadential coda. There is a similar coda in Ricercar [11].

The harmony in Padovano's ricercars is probably their weakest element.[63] At times there are long passages (Ricercar [12], mm. 61-127,[64] and Ricercar [14], mm. 28-38) in which the harmonic rhythm is broad and slow-moving. Padovano used dissonance with less frequency and imagination than did Willaert or Segni in their *Musica Nova* ricercars.

Although Padovano used the old system of eight church modes, some interesting exceptions to normal procedure indicate that this composer was seeking to expand the existing tonal system. Ricercar [12] "del Secondo Tono" and Ricercar [14] "del Quinto Tono" have a key signature of one flat indicating a transposition of the mode up a fourth. The former work, with its final on g, is indeed a transposition; however, the final cadence of Ricercar [14] is on f, normally the final for the untransposed mode V.[65] Another curious aspect of Padovano's use of tonality occurs in Ricercar [11] "del Primo Tono." This work, whose tonality is untransposed mode I, has a greater number of cadences on its dominant, a, than on its basic tonal center of d.

Padovano's most radical experiment in expanding the old system of church modes occurs in Ricercar [15]. The 1556 publication of this ricercar shows a set of two clef signs and a key signature of either three or four sharps in each of the four voice parts. Example 7 below reproduces the incipits of each voice part.

Ex. 7. Double clef signs and key signatures at the beginning of Padovano's "Ricercar del Primo Tono" [15], reproduced from No. IX of *Il Primo Libro de Ricercari*, 1556.

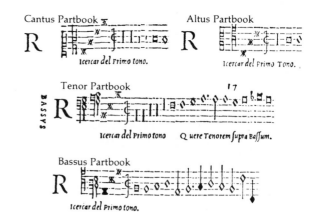

This ricercar was transcribed in the Pierront and Hennebains edition (1934) according to the first set of clefs, namely: first-line c for the Cantus, third-line c for the Altus, fourth-line c for the Tenor (Bassus partbook), and fourth-line f for the

Bass (Tenor partbook). The possible significance of the key signature was totally ignored.[66]

The double clef signs and the key signature seem to indicate that Padovano intended two possible methods of performance of Ricercar [15] "del Primo Tono." For the most obvious method of performance the music would be read according to the first set of clefs, the *chiavi naturali*,[67] disregarding the key signature; this method is used in the Pierront and Hennebains edition. With its final on d, this reading would be in untransposed mode I. The second way of performing the piece would be to read according to the second set of clefs, called the *low chiavette*, thereby transposing the mode I tonality from d down a minor third to b. In order to make this transposition correctly, however, it is necessary to have a key signature of f-sharp, c-sharp, and g-sharp. This ricercar has the c-sharp and g-sharp in its key signature when read from the *low chiavette*, but the f-sharp is lacking. It seems logical that the performer was expected to supply, when necessary, the missing f-sharp in the key signature.[68] For purposes of comparison, two readings of the same passage from Ricercar [15] "del Primo Tono" are shown in Example 8, one according to the *chiavi naturali*, the other according to the *low chiavette*.

Ex. 8. Padovano, "Ricercar del Primo Tono" [15], mm. 13-16. Two readings compared: (a) according to the *chiavi naturali*, in mode I, d tonality; (b) according to the *low chiavette*, in mode I, transposed to b tonality.

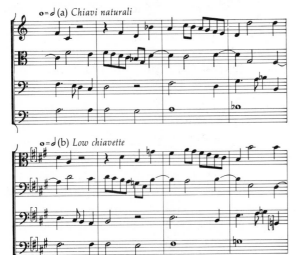

A problem arises concerning the g-flat accidentals that occur when reading the music from the *low chiavette*, but it is easily solved by remembering that the flat sign was used instead of the natural sign by sixteenth-century composers to cancel a sharp in the key signature. Hence, as is shown in Example 8, the g-flat accidentals in measures 14 and 16 that occur when reading from the *low chiavette* should be interpreted as natural signs canceling the g-sharp in the key signature.

The procedure outlined above results in a satisfactory reading of Ricercar [15] according to the *low chiavette*, in mode I transposed to the uncommon (in the sixteenth century) tonality of b. This is not the only time Padovano used an unusual tonality for his ricercars; one of his keyboard works, "Ricercar del Sesto Tono Alla Terza," in the 1604 publication, is written in the key of "D major."[69]

Padovano and Malvezzi were both master contrapuntists. Their styles differ in many respects, however. Padovano's ricercars were written in the grand manner of Willaert's Venetian School, with its emphasis on intricate counterpoint, conservative harmonic treatment, and flowing melodic lines. The use of Gregorian chant melodies is one of the most important features of Padovano's music. His experiments in expanding the modal system of his day represent a progressive stylistic aspect that was to become even more apparent in his later works. Certainly the popularity of Padovano's music long after his death is testimony to the importance and high esteem accorded him in the late sixteenth century. Malvezzi's ricercar style inclines less toward the architectural formalism of the Renaissance. Instead it emphasizes the nervous, experimental characteristics of the early baroque. In art history this style and period of transition is aptly called mannerism. Manneristic elements of Malvezzi's style are: (1) use of motivic themes, often in stretto; (2) irregular opening and subsequent expositions; (3) frequent contrasts in rhythmic, harmonic, and contrapuntal movement and texture; and (4) experiments with chromaticism.

Peri's style as a contrapuntist, necessarily based as it is on an analysis of just one ricercar composed when he was but seventeen years of age, exhibits some similarities to Malvezzi's style. There are also significant differences between Peri's and Malvezzi's styles, among which are absence of theme modification, transparent contrapuntal texture, and conservative use of chromaticism in Peri's ricercar. These departures from the style of his teacher as well as his contrapuntal skill mark Jacopo Peri "il Zazzerino" as an independent young composer worthy of encouragement.

Padovano's ricercars still typify the Renaissance style of the Venetian School, while those of the

Florentines Malvezzi and Peri constitute a manneristic bridge from the Venetian Renaissance to the early baroque, particularly the style of composers working in Southern Italy. The fact that these ricercars delineate this transition in the field of instrumental music emphasizes their historical significance. Moreover, the aesthetic qualities of several of the pieces mark them as true monuments of music.

## Performance Practice

The function for which these ricercars were composed is not indicated in any of the sources, nor do the extant sixteenth- and seventeenth-century accounts of Italian musical life furnish specific information. The outward polyphonic resemblance of the ricercar to the motet, the fact that many ricercar composers were church musicians, and Frescobaldi's use of the ricercar in his set of organ Masses *(Fiori Musicali)* lead to the assumption that the ricercar was primarily used as church music. However, although many keyboard ricercars were used in the church, it is likely that ensemble ricercars were intended to be performed as chamber music either at meetings of the many academies and *scuoli grandi* that flourished throughout Italy during the sixteenth century[70] or in the homes of the wealthy nobility.

None of the title pages of the source publications indicates the intended medium of performance, although the publishing of these ricercars in partbooks clearly denotes ensemble performance of some kind. Title pages of several ensemble ricercar publications even as far back as *Musica Nova* (1540) specify "Accommodata per cantar et sonar sopra organi; et altri strumenti" (Suitable for singing and playing on the organ and other instruments). A full consort of viols, winds, or voices might be employed, or the instruments could be mixed depending on what was available. Vocal performance would have been accomplished by use of Guido d'Arezzo's solmization syllables together with his system of hexachords; this method of singing without words was still popular in the sixteenth century. For a performance on the organ or on other keyboard instruments it would have been necessary to copy the parts off onto a score; it was no doubt precisely for this purpose that manuscript scores were made of Padovano's and Malvezzi's publications. The primary concern of composer, performer, and listener alike was the artistic contrapuntal treatment of themes in the ricercars; the performing medium was of little consequence.

Evidence that at least some rules of *musica ficta* were commonly observed in the performance of late sixteenth-century music exists in an interesting aspect of Malvezzi's notation. In Ricercar [7] (measure 33) both the print and the manuscript have a sharp sign preceding the b in the Altus part on the fourth beat (see Example 9).

Ex. 9. Malvezzi, Ricercar [7], mm. 33-34 (Altus)

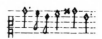

Since it is impossible that this pitch could be interpreted as b-sharp here, the sharp accidental must therefore be interpreted as a natural sign, making the pitch b-natural.[71] But this interpretation seems questionable since, according to modern notation, the natural sign here is superfluous. However, viewed in sixteenth-century terms, the natural sign is quite necessary. An examination of the Altus passage here (see Example 9) reveals that the progression leads from a up to the b-natural and then down a major third to g. According to the rules of *musica ficta*, the b in a progression like this should be lowered a half-step in performance. Therefore, it seems evident that Malvezzi added this "superfluous" accidental precisely in order to prevent the application of *musica ficta* at this point.

The ranges of the four voice parts in each of the fifteen ricercars are indicated on the music pages of this edition at the beginning of the pieces. Suggested viol and modern string instrumentations for Ricercars [1]-[5] and [10]-[14] are as follows: treble viol, tenor viol, tenor viol, and bass viol; violin, viola, viola, and violoncello. Suggested instrumentations for the remaining pieces are:

Ricercar [6]   Viols: treble, tenor, tenor, bass
Modern Strings: violin, viola, violoncello, violoncello

Ricercar [7]   Viols: treble, treble, tenor, tenor
Modern Strings: violin, violin, viola, violoncello (or viola)

Ricercar [8]   Viols: treble, treble, tenor, bass
Modern Strings: violin, violin, viola, violoncello

Ricercar [9]   Viols: treble, treble, tenor, bass
Modern Strings: violin, violin, viola, violoncello

Ricercar [15]   Viols: tenor, tenor, bass, bass
Modern Strings: viola, violoncello, violoncello, violoncello

Instrumentation of the parts for Ricercar [15] is given according to the transcription of this piece in *low chiavette*. Other instruments or voices may be substituted for those suggested above so long as the range of the substituted voice or instrument matches that of the part. The solmization system described above, with a mutation or transition from one hexachord to another when necessary, is still appropriate for modern vocal performance of the ricercars.[72]

## The Edition

### Sources

Malvezzi's and Peri's ricercars are found in a print issued in 1577 and in a manuscript copy of that print catalogued as Florence Ms. Mus. II.I.295. Padovano's Ricercars [11] through [14] of the present edition exist in four sources: a 1556 print, a 1588 reprint, Florence Ms. Mus. II.I.295, and Brussels MS 26661. Ricercar [15] by Padovano appears in the 1556 print, the 1588 reprint, and the Brussels manuscript. Each of these prints and manuscripts is discussed below.

The title page of the 1577 print reads: DI CRISTOFANO / MALVEZZI DA LVCCA, MAESTRO / DI CAPELLA DEL SERENISSIMO / GRAN DVCA DI TOSCANA. / IL PRIMO LIBRO DE RECERCARI [sic] / à Quattro Voci, Nuouamente da lui / Composti, & dati in luce. / CAN [printer's device] TVS / IN PERVGIA, / Appresso Pietroiacomo Petrucci, l' Anno. 1577. (By Cristofano Malvezzi of Lucca, Master of the Chapel of the most Serene Grand Duke of Tuscany. First Book of Ricercars for four voices, newly composed by him and put in print. Cantus. In Perugia, published by Pietroiacomo Petrucci, the year 1577.) The ten ensemble ricercars in this print were published as a set of four partbooks (Cantus, Altus, Tenor, and Bass). The title page of the Altus part is reproduced in Plate I. The dedication, printed on the second folio of the publication, refers to the famous Count Bardi of the Florentine *Camerata*: "Al Molto Illustre Signore Giovanni de Bardi De Conti di Vernio."

A copy of this publication is located at the Civico Museo Bibliografico Musicale in Bologna.[73] The inscription "Di Niccolo Berlini" (probably the name of a former owner) exists on the title page of each partbook, and several additional inscriptions (including the words "Corus Angelorum" and some graffiti) appear on the table-of-contents page of the Tenor partbook. Unfortunately, this unique source is incomplete and a reconstruction of Malvezzi's ricercars from it, alone,

is impossible. The Bass partbook is lost and pages six through thirteen are missing in both the Cantus and Tenor partbooks.

A catalog of the music manuscripts in the Biblioteca nazionale, Florence, published in 1959 by Bianca Becherini[74] describes a manuscript in the Magliabecchi collection designated as Florence Ms. Mus. II.I.295 in which all of Malvezzi's ricercars have been copied.[75] This manuscript copy was used, along with the surviving fragments of the 1577 print, to transcribe the first ten ensemble ricercars in the present edition.[76] Florence Ms. Mus. II.I.295 is thirty-six and one-half centimeters high by twenty-five centimeters wide, and it contains fifty-four unnumbered folios. The pages each have sixteen staves; there are four systems of music in four-part open score. Each page is divided into twelve equally-spaced measures with the barlines drawn as unbroken lines from the top to the bottom of the page before the music was written. Each system of music reads straight across from the left-hand page (folio verso, ᵛ) to the right-hand page (folio recto, ʳ).

The manuscript contains four ricercars (folios 1ᵛ-9) recently discovered to be by Padovano, copied from his publication of 1556 (Ricercars [11]-[14] of the present edition); ten ricercars by Jacques Buus, copied from his *Ricercari da Cantare e Sonare ... Libro Primo*, 1547 (folios 8ᵛ-38ᵛ); and the ten ricercars copied from Malvezzi's publication of 1577 (folios 38ᵛ-50). The remainder of the manuscript (folios 51-54ᵛ) contains eight pages of unidentified music in a different handwriting from that appearing in the main portion of the manuscript. The only mark of identification on the manuscript is the inscription of Malvezzi's name at the beginning of his works. The style of writing indicates that most of Florence Ms. Mus. II.I.295 was probably written in the last years of the sixteenth century; the last pages were added by another hand in the early seventeenth century.[77]

A comparison of the Florence manuscript with Malvezzi's 1577 print reveals some interesting characteristics, several of which are exhibited in Example 10 (see following page). It is evident that the copyist used many tied notes not only over the barline, but within the measure as well. For instance, notes shown in the print as semibreves are notated by the copyist in every case as two minims tied together (see Example 10, a). Sometimes the copyist ties four minims together, all within the same measure, to represent a notated breve in the print; the ties in every case connect the stems of the notes rather than their heads.

Ex. 10. Malvezzi, Ricercar [7], mm. 31-46 and mm. 55-64, reproduced from Florence Ms. Mus. II.I.295, f. 45ᵛ-46, section of the third and fourth systems.

Sharp signs are found below the note or even below the staff (see Example 10, b). These are not *musica ficta* alterations added by the manuscript copyist; a comparison of the manuscript with the surviving fragments of the print shows that every sharp sign in the manuscript is accounted for in the print. The copyist probably placed the sharp sign below the note because of a lack of space. The smaller flat sign, on the other hand, is always placed next to the note on the staff.

The ricercar by Peri that is included in the present edition was, until recently, thought to be one of Malvezzi's pieces. Ricercar [9] of Malvezzi's 1577 publication is entitled "Ricercar del Primo Tuono Del Zazzerino." At first the meaning of "Zazzerino" was a mystery, but, as has been mentioned above, "Zazzerino" names the composer (Peri) rather than the title of Ricercar [9]. This phenomenon leads to the belief that Ricercar [9] is a heretofore unknown work by Peri.[78] Because it was included in Malvezzi's 1577 print, Peri's ricercar also appears in the manuscript copy of the 1577 publication, Florence Ms. Mus. II.I.295.

The five ricercars by Padovano appearing in the present edition were first published in 1556 as part of a set of thirteen ensemble ricercars. The title page of the 1556 print, issued as a set of four partbooks in mensural notation, reads: CANTVS / DI ANNIBALE / PADOVANO, ORGANISTA / Della Illustrissima .S. di Venetia in San Marco, Il Primo / Nuouamente Libro de Ricercari a quatro uoci, Nuouamente da / lui composti, & dati in

luce. / A QVATTRO [*printers device*] VOCI / In Venetia apresso di / Antonio Gardano / 1556. (By Annibale Padovano, organist of the Most Illustrious Signori of Venice in St. Mark's, the First Book of Ricercars for four voices, newly composed by him, and put in print. For four voices, in Venice published by Antonio Gardano 1556.) (See Plate III.) The only extant copy of the 1556 print is in the library of the Royal College of Music, London.

In 1588, thirteen years after Padovano's death, Angelo Gardano published a reprint of these thirteen ensemble ricercars, with the title page reading: ALTO / DI ANNIBALE PADOVANO / ORGANISTA DELLA SERENISS. SIG. DI VENETIA. / IL PRIMO LIBRO DE RICERCARI / A QVATTRO VOCI, / Nouamente Ristampato. / [*printer's device*] / In Venetia, Appresso Angelo Gardano. / M. D. LXXXVIII. (By Annibale Padovano organist of the most serene signori of Venice. The first book of ricercars for four voices, newly reprinted. In Venice, published by Angelo Gardano. 1588.) (See Plate III.) Just one copy of the reprint (also published in partbooks) has survived, and it is not complete: the Cantus and Bass partbooks are missing. The Alto and Tenor partbooks are located at the Civico Museo Bibliografico Musicale in Bologna, and with the exception of a few obvious printing errors, the surviving music of the 1588 reprint corresponds exactly with that of the 1556 edition.[79]

As has been mentioned above, Padovano's Ricercars [11]–[14] of the present edition are the first four ensemble ricercars of Florence Ms. Mus. II.I.295. Folios 1ᵛ–9 contain the four imitative works without designation of any kind, and, until recently, they have been of unknown authorship. However, a comparison of the incipits of these pieces with those in a catalog of ricercar opening themes compiled by the present editor has revealed that these four ensemble ricercars are by Annibale Padovano, and taken from his publication of 1556; comparison with the 1556 publication has verified this authorship.

Another manuscript containing Padovano's ricercars, located in the Bibliothèque du Conservatoire de Bruxelles (MS 26661), testifies to the popularity of this composer long after his death in 1575. Made by an anonymous musician probably early in the seventeenth century, the title page of this manuscript reads: Le quattro parte, / Di Annibale Padovano, Organista / della Illustrisse .S. di Venetia / in San Marco, il Primo / Libro de Ricercari à quattro / voci, nouamente da lui composti, / et dati in luce. / In Venetia appresso di /

## TABLE 1.

### Collation of Annibale Padovano's Ensemble Ricercars

as they appear in the various prints, manuscripts, and modern editions

| Annibale Padovano, Il Primo Libro de Ricercari, 1556 | Annibale Padovano, Il Primo Libro de Ricercari, 1588 | Brussels MS 26661 | Florence Ms. Mus. II.I.295 | V. Galilei, Fronimo Dialogo, 1584 (lute tablature) | G. Fallamero, Intavolatura da Liuto, 1584 | S. Bertoldo, Tocate Ricercari et Canzoni Francese, 1591 (organ tablature) | Pierront and Hennebains, ed., 1934 | Swenson, ed., 1977 |
|---|---|---|---|---|---|---|---|---|
| I. Ricercar del Terzo Tono | No. 1 | No. 1, p. 1 | No. 3, f. 5ᵛ | — | — | No. 5, p. 20 | No. 1 | [13] |
| II. Ricercar del Settimo Tono | No. 2 | No. 2, p. 7 | — | No. 2, p. 4 | — | — | No. 2 | — |
| III. Ricercar del Sesto Tono | No. 3 | No. 3, p. 13 | — | — | — | — | No. 3 | — |
| IV. Ricercar del Primo Tono | No. 4 | No. 4, p. 18 | No. 1, f. 1ᵛ | — | — | No. 4, p. 15 | No. 4 | [11] |
| V. Ricercar del Secondo Tono | No. 5 | No. 5, p. 25 | No. 2, f. 2ᵛ | — | — | — | No. 5 | [12] |
| VI. Ricercar del Ottavo Tono | No. 6 | No. 6, p. 34 | — | — | — | — | No. 6 | — |
| VII. Ricercar del Primo Tono | No. 7 | No. 7, p. 38 | — | — | — | — | No. 7 | — |
| VIII. Ricercar del Ottavo Tono | No. 8 | No. 8, p. 45 | — | — | No. 42, p. 69 | — | No. 8 | — |
| IX. Ricercar del Primo Tono (double set of clefs) | No. 9 | No. 9, p. 50 | — | — | — | — | No. 9 (Chiavi Naturali) | [15] (Low Chiavette) |
| X. Ricercar del Quinto Tono | No. 10 | No. 10, p. 56 | No. 4, f. 7ᵛ | — | — | — | No. 10 | [14] |
| XI. Ricercar del Terzo Tono | No. 11 | No. 11, p. 61 | — | — | No. 41, p. 65 | — | No. 11 | — |
| XII. Ricercar del Terzo Tono | No. 12 | No. 12, p. 66 | — | — | — | — | No. 12 | — |
| XIII. Ricercar del Sesto Tono | No. 13 | No. 13, p. 71 | — | — | — | — | No. 13 | — |

Antonio Gardano / 1556. Immediately after the title page there is a dedication page followed by a manuscript copy in partitura score of Padovano's thirteen ensemble ricercars.[80]

There are seventy-five pages of music in the Brussels manuscript, with the page number appearing in the upper outside corner of each page. On page 75 at the end of the last ricercar there is inscribed: ▲ LAVS ▲ DEO ▲ (Praise the Lord). On each page there are eighteen staves with four systems of music in four-part open score; two of the staves are unused. Between each system a heavy, wavy horizontal line is drawn for the purpose of separation. Each page is divided into eleven equally spaced measures, with the barlines drawn from the top to the bottom of the page before the music was notated. Each measure of the Brussels manuscript contains one semibreve or its equivalent; in the Florence manuscript each measure contains the equivalent of a breve. Also unlike the Florence manuscript, tied notes (tied at the stems rather than at the heads) occur in the

Brussels manuscript only where the barline makes a tie necessary.

A comparison of the 1556 print, the 1588 reprint, and the Brussels manuscript reveals that, with the exception of the first line in the manuscript, "Le quattro parte," the title and dedication pages of the 1556 print and the Brussels manuscript are exactly the same. The 1588 reprint, on the other hand, has no dedication page, and its title page differs in several respects from the original print and from the Brussels manuscript. That the works in the Brussels manuscript were copied from the 1556 print rather than from the later reprint is evidenced not only by the obvious similarity of title pages including the date, but also by the fact that the few printing errors occurring in the 1588 reprint do not appear in the manuscript.

The final ricercar in the present edition appears in Padovano's 1556 print (it is labeled *IX, Ricercar del Primo Tono*), in the 1588 reprint, and in the Brussels manuscript. Its notation in all of the sources is unique. Example 7, above, shows the sets of two clef signs and the unusual key signature in the different voice parts. Also shown in this example are the opening measures in the Tenor partbook where the inscriptions "BASSVS" and "Quere Tenorem supra Bassum" indicate that the "Bassus" voice part is printed in the Tenor partbook, while the Tenor voice part is found in place of the Bass, or in the Bass partbook. The present editor has transcribed the piece according to these directions.

One keyboard and two lute publications containing intabulated versions of several of Padovano's ricercars appeared in the last two decades of the sixteenth century. Organ transcriptions of Ricercars I and IV from the 1556 edition appear in Sperindio Bertoldo's keyboard publication of 1591.[81] An intabulation for lute of Ricercar II from the 1556 edition is in Vincenzo Galilei's *Fronimo Dialogo*, dated 1584.[82] Two other pieces from the 1556 edition, Ricercars VIII and XI, also existed as lute transcriptions in Gabriel Fallamero's *Il Primo Libro de Intavolatura da Liuto* (1584).[83]

A modern edition (1934) of Padovano's ensemble ricercars was edited by Pierront and Hennebains.[84] However, this publication cannot be cited as a definitive edition as it treats these ensemble ricercars solely as organ pieces. A collation of Padovano's ensemble ricercars as they appear in the various partbook prints, manuscripts, lute and keyboard intabulations, the Pierront and Hennebains edition, and the present edition is shown in Table 1 on the previous page.

## Editorial Methods

Malvezzi's and Peri's ricercars were prepared for this edition from the surviving fragments of Malvezzi's 1577 publication; missing portions were supplied from the Florence Ms. Mus. II.I.295. Ricercars [1]–[10] of the present edition appear in the same order in which they were in the 1577 print.

Ricercars [11]–[14] by Padovano have been transcribed from the 1556 print (they are numbered IV, V, I, and X there) and from Florence Ms. Mus. II.I.295. Padovano's Ricercar [15] has the 1556 publication as its source. All of these transcriptions were also checked against the 1588 reprint.

The present transcription of music from Malvezzi's 1577 publication has been checked with a transcription made by the late Hans David. A better edition has resulted from this opportunity because in a number of places the Florence manuscript is almost illegible. Each of Dr. David's contributions is recorded in the Critical Notes.

Original clefs, key signature, the mensuration sign, and the first note of each part in its original value are shown in the incipits at the beginning of each piece. The scale of reduction is 2:1, meaning that a half-note in the sources has been reduced to a quarter-note in the transcriptions. Although the partbooks of the original publications do not use barlines, barlines do exist in the manuscript score. In the Florence manuscript barlines mark the passage of each imperfect breve in duple mensuration and each perfect or dotted breve in triple mensuration. The barring is different in the Brussels manuscript where each measure contains a semibreve. The present edition follows the Florence manuscript (taking into account the 2:1 reduction) in that there is barring for every whole-note (duple meter) or dotted whole-note (triple meter). Meter signatures used in the edition correspond exactly to those found in the sources.

The final notes of each piece, shown as longas in the sources, have been written as whole-notes with fermatas in the present edition. In some of the works (Ricercars [3] Tenor, [4] Cantus, [7] Cantus, [8] Cantus, [10] Tenor, [11] Altus), one of the voice parts ends several measures before the other parts do. In these cases the composer obviously intended the final longa of the shortened voice part to be held through the final cadence as a pedal point with all four parts ending together. This is accomplished in the present edition by tying the affected note through the remaining measures of the piece. *Punctus divisionis* and coloration were used in the sources to define rhythm in the triple-meter sections of Ricercars [4], [8], and [11]. In the present edition this is indicated by the sign ⌐ ¬ placed above the staff.

Brackets enclose editorial additions, while editorial corrections and alterations are incorporated in the transcriptions and recorded in the Critical Notes. Accidentals have been notated according to modern practice, and all redundant accidentals have been removed, although recorded in the Critical Notes. Where a sharp or a flat sign has been used in the sources to cancel a previously flatted or sharped note, a natural sign has been substituted. Cautionary accidentals placed in parentheses have been added to make clear the limited influence of certain original accidentals. All other editorial accidentals have been placed above the staff, over the note being altered; these editorial accidentals affect only the notes over which they have been placed.

In the present edition, just as with any modern edition of Renaissance music, the problems of *musica ficta* are ever present. Although *musica ficta* was certainly a part of sixteenth-century performance practice, a wide degree of latitude must have existed—depending on performers, time, and place—in the interpretation and application of the rules of this largely unwritten tradition. For these reasons the present editor has been conservative in adding *musica ficta* accidentals; the performer may make his own decisions. In those few places where a *musica ficta* alteration was considered necessary, the editorial accidental has been placed above the staff.

There are a number of errors in Florence Ms. Mus. II.I.295 that posed some transcribing difficulties; several of these are illustrated in Example 10. For instance, in the Bass part the measure designated as (c)—measure 38 of Ricercar [7]—has the equivalent of five minims, there being one minim too many. This copyist error causes a shift of the Bass part one minim's-worth to the left from this point on, as is indicated by the small vertical lines superimposed by the editor above the Bass. A measure with only three minims'-worth in the Bass part several measures later (not shown in Example 10) rectifies this shift. The Cantus part also exhibits several shifts. At the beginning of Example 10 the Cantus part has already been shifted one minim's-worth, as is indicated by the small vertical lines. Then at (d), measure 32, a missing minim-rest causes an additional one-minim's-worth shift of the Cantus.

This shift continues until (e), measure 55, in which there is the equivalent of five minims; now there is a total shift of three minims'-worth. Finally, another five-minim measure at (f), measure 62, adds one more minim's-worth to the Cantus shift which now totals a full measure. These shifts in the Cantus part continue until the end of the piece. This type of copying error is quite common throughout the manuscript; it occurs in all but the first and last of the ten ricercars copied from Malvezzi's print. It is difficult to believe that the manuscript copyist was more than a student; otherwise most of these errors would have been detected during transcription by reading all the parts together.

*Critical Notes*

These notes refer to discrepancies between the present edition of Malvezzi's and Peri's ricercars and the source material of Malvezzi's 1577 print, Florence Ms. Mus. II.I.295, and Hans David's transcription. The notes also record discrepancies between the present edition of Padovano's ricercars and the source material of the 1556 print, the 1588 reprint, Florence Ms. Mus. II.I.295, and the Brussels manuscript. Abbreviations for source material are as follows: Fl.Ms. = Florence Ms. Mus. II.I.295; 1577 = Malvezzi's 1577 print; 1556 = 1556 print; 1588 = 1588 reprint; Br.Ms. = Brussels MS 26661; D. = Hans David's transcription. C., A., T., B. indicate Cantus, Altus, Tenor, and Bass. The usual pitch designations are used where middle C = c′, two-line C = c″, and so forth. Sm. = semiminim, mi. = minim, sb. = semibreve, br. = breve.

RICERCAR [1]—M. 29, B., notes 2-3, Fl.Ms. not clear as to tied or repeated notes; D. transcribes repeated notes. M. 43, A., note 10 is c′ in Fl.Ms. and e′ in 1577. M. 54, B., notes 1-2, Fl.Ms. not clear as to tied or repeated notes; D. transcribes repeated notes. M. 84, A., note 6 is sb. followed by a dot in 1577 and a mi. in Fl.Ms.

RICERCAR [2]—M. 20, C., note 1, sb.-rest inserted before the f′ in Fl.Ms., thus shifting the Cantus part two minims'-worth from here to m. 34. M. 25, A., note 4, sources show redundant flat sign. M. 26, A., note 1 is e′ in 1577 and Fl.Ms. M. 34, C., note 1 is a sb. instead of a br. in Fl.Ms., thereby compensating for the previous error in m. 20. M. 47, A., Fl.Ms. reads sb.-rest, mi. (f), mi. (g), mi. (a), mi. (b-flat), sb. (d′). M. 49, B., note 4 is d in Fl.Ms. M. 56, B., notes 4-5 are c and G in Fl. Ms. M. 84, C., note 6 is a′ tied over in Fl.Ms. and f′ tied over in 1577. M. 97, A., notes 3-4 are tied together in Fl.Ms. Mm. 103-104, T., these measures are as follows in Fl.Ms.:

RICERCAR [3]—M. 8, A., note 1 shifted back into m. 7, thus giving m. 7 five minims'-worth and shifting A. part one minim's-worth in Fl.Ms. M. 9, A., Fl.Ms. shows:

The incorrect notes (bracketed) compensate for the previous error. M. 28, T., note 3 is sm. in 1577 and mi. in Fl.Ms. M. 36, B., note 4 is unclear in Fl.Ms., D. transcribes B-flat. M. 58, B., notes 2-3, tie is omitted in Fl.Ms. which shows a slur from the sm. g to the following fusa f. M. 62, B., Fl.Ms. omits the rest in this measure. M. 65, note 8, m. 66, note 1, T., these notes are sm. in 1577 and Fl.Ms. and there is a subsequent shift of the T. part from here on. M. 67, B., note 3, sources show redundant flat sign. M. 71, T., beat 2 has mi.-rest in Fl.Ms. and the T. part is shifted an additional minim's-worth from here on.

RICERCAR [4]—M. 7, T., note 4, sources show redundant sharp sign. M. 38, C., note 1, C. part of 1577 missing from here on. M. 39, T., note 3, sources show redundant sharp sign. M. 47, T., note 3, T. part of 1577 missing from here on. M. 49, B., note 1, Fl.Ms. has an additional sb. on g repeated from m. 48, shifting the B. part from here to m. 95. M. 68, T., note 1 is omitted in Fl.Ms. causing the T. part to be shifted from here to m. 97, D. interpolates the note b here. M. 87, B., note 5, sources show redundant flat sign. M. 95, B., sb.-rest here in Fl.Ms. compensates for previous error in M. 49. M. 97, T., note 4 is followed by sb.-rest in Fl.Ms. thus compensating for the previous error in m. 68. M. 105, T., note 3, pitch is not clear in Fl.Ms.; D. transcribes it as e'. M. 111, T., despite the *punctus divisionis* appearing above the staff, the Fl.Ms. incorrectly shows the br. as imperfect, with the following br. (on f) coming in on the third beat of this measure; hence the T. part is shifted from here on. M. 124, T., note 1 is an imperfect br. in Fl.Ms. and the T. part is shifted an additional beat from here on. M. 125, note 2–end, B., Fl.Ms. shows this part as follows:

M. 127, A., note 4, sources show redundant sharp sign; T., note 1 written as an imperfect br. in Fl.Ms. and the T. part is shifted an additional minim's-worth. The three errors in the T. part in m. 111, m. 124, and m. 127 effect a total shift of three minims'-worth causing the final note of the T. to come in 1 measure too soon in Fl.Ms.

RICERCAR [5]—M. 8, C., note 3, sources show redundant sharp sign. M. 22, C., note 3, sources show redundant sharp sign. M. 29, A., note 3, sources show redundant sharp sign. M. 48, T. part in Fl.Ms. has five minims'-worth in this measure and the T. is shifted from here on. M. 50, T., Fl.Ms. shows a mi.-rest instead of a sb.-rest in this measure, hence the T. is shifted an additional minim's-worth from here to m. 85. M. 77, A., note 6, sources show redundant sharp sign. M. 85, T., note 1 is sm. in Fl.Ms., hence the T. part is shifted one additional minim's-worth from here on. M. 87, T., Fl.Ms. shows only three minims'-worth in this measure, thus partially compensating for previous shifts in the T. part. M. 91, T., Fl.Ms. shows only 3½ minims'-worth in this measure, thus partially compensating for previous shifts in the T. part. M. 93, T., note 4 is sm. in Fl.Ms., thus partially compensating for previous shifts in T. part. M. 97, A., Fl.Ms. has dotted mi. (b), sm. (c'), mi. (d'), mi. (f'); present edition follows 1577.

RICERCAR [6]—M. 7, C., this measure has five minims'-worth in Fl.Ms., hence the C. part is shifted one beat from here on. M. 35, C., note 1 is a mi. in Fl.Ms., D.'s transcription appears in the present edition; B., beat 2, br.-rest here in Fl.Ms. M. 52, T., note 2 is a fusa in Fl.Ms. M. 55, C., beat 1, Fl.Ms. omits mi.-rest and C. part is shifted one additional minim's-worth from here on. M. 66, A., an additional sm. (b-flat) interpolated before note 1 in Fl.Ms.

RICERCAR [7]—M. 4, T., note 3 not clear in Fl.Ms., D. suggests two tied minims on e' transcribed here as a half-note. M. 18, A., note 2, sources show redundant sharp sign. M. 19, T., Fl.Ms. not clear in this measure, the present edition adopts D.'s solution. M. 27, C. part in this measure has five minims'-worth in Fl.Ms. and the C. part is shifted one minim's-worth from here on. M. 33, C., Fl.Ms. omits the mi.-rest, hence the C. part is shifted an additional minim's-worth from here to m. 55. M. 38, A., note 4, sources show redundant sharp sign; B. part in this measure has five minims'-worth in Fl.Ms. and the B. part is shifted one minim's-worth from here on. M. 42, B. part has only three minims'-worth in this measure in Fl.Ms. thus compensating for the previous shift of m. 38. M. 48, C., note 1, part not clear here in Fl.Ms. M. 52, B., second half of beat 1, part not clear here in Fl.Ms., D.'s solution of the quarter-rest is adopted here. M. 55, C. part has five minims'-worth in this measure in Fl.Ms., hence the Cantus is shifted one additional minim's-worth from here to m. 62. M. 61, A. part in this measure has four mi. tied together in Fl.Ms., the present edition follows 1577. M. 62, C. part has five minims'-worth in this measure in Fl.Ms., hence the C. part is shifted an additional minim's-worth from here on; the accumulated shift is now one full measure. M. 70, C., notes 6-9 are not clear here in Fl.Ms., D.'s transcription is adopted in the present edition. M. 73, C., the rest in this measure is omitted in Fl.Ms. and the previous shifts in the C. part are partially compensated for. M. 77, C., notes 1-2, an additional mi. (e'') is interpolated between these notes in Fl.Ms. shifting the C. part an additional minim's-worth. M. 88, A., note 8, sources show redundant sharp sign. M. 91, C., notes 5 and 6 are not clear in Fl.Ms., D.'s transcription is adopted in the present edition. M. 92, C., note 3, sources show redundant sharp sign. M. 97, C., note 3, sources show redundant sharp sign.

RICERCAR [8]—Incipit, B., as shown here, Fl.Ms. incorrectly uses the F-clef on the fourth line of the staff instead of on the third line. This error is corrected on f. 47ᵛ. M. 32, C., rhythm is unclear in this measure in Fl.Ms., D. shows:

♩ ♫♫♪ ♪♩ ♪|

M. 36, C. part shows only two minims'-worth in this measure in Fl.Ms. and so the C. part is shifted two minims'-worth from here on. Mm. 38-40, C. part in Fl.Ms. has only 3½ minims'-worth in m. 38 and 4½ minims'-worth in m. 39. M. 41, C., beats 3-4, sb.-rest is omitted in Fl.Ms. and this compensates for the previous shift of m. 36 of the C. part. M. 49, T., notes 1 and 2 are tied in Fl.Ms. M. 52, A. part shows five minims'-worth in this measure in Fl.Ms., hence the part is shifted one minim's-worth from here to m. 69. M. 59, T., notes 4-5 are c' and b-flat in Fl.Ms. M. 62, C., D. suggests the *musica ficta* accidentals presented here. M. 69, A., beat 4, Fl.Ms. shows a mi. a' interpolated at the end of the measure thereby compensating for the previous shift in m. 52 of the A. part. M. 80, A., note 3, tie omitted in Fl.Ms., the present edition reflects 1577. M. 87, C., note 1, Fl.Ms. shows this br. as imperfect, with the penultimate note of the C. part (d'') beginning on the third beat of this measure, and not

resolving to the final c'' until the last measure. M. 88, B., beat 3, Fl.Ms. is unclear here. M. 90, C., note 1 is d'' tied to d'' of preceding measure in Fl.Ms.

RICERCAR [9]—M. 18, C., note 5, printed edition (1577) of C. part resumes here. M. 27, A., note 4 is g' in Fl.Ms. M. 28, C., rest is a mi.-rest in 1577 and Fl.Ms. causing a one-minim's-worth shift from here to m. 37; as D. suggests, the rest should be a sb. M. 34, T., note 3, printed edition (1577) of T. part resumes here. M. 37, C., Fl.Ms. reads sm. (b'-flat), sm. (c''), mi. (d''), mi. (d'') for this measure and omits the sb.-rest, hence the C. part is shifted one additional minim's-worth from here to m. 60. M. 57, B., rest 1 is omitted in Fl.Ms. and the B. part is shifted two minims'-worth from here to m. 79. M. 60, C., Fl.Ms. adds a sb.-rest at the end of this measure, thereby fully compensating for the previous shifts in the C. part in mm. 27 and 37. M. 70, T., note 1 is b'-flat in Fl.Ms. M. 72, T., note 1, D. suggests the *musica ficta* flat. M. 79, B., Fl.Ms. shows two mi. (g-f) at the end of the measure; they are omitted here at D.'s suggestion to correct the previous shift in m. 57.

RICERCAR [10]—Incipit, B., Fl.Ms. incorrectly shows the F-clef on the third line of the staff instead of the fourth line. The error is corrected on f. 49ᵛ. M. 25, C. shows a G-clef sign here in Fl.Ms.; C. and B. parts have one-flat key signature on last system of f. 48ᵛ of Fl.Ms.; A. part shows a C-clef on the second line of the staff instead of the third on last system of f. 48ᵛ of Fl.Ms. M. 40, C., note 3, sources show redundant sharp sign.

RICERCAR [11]—M. 10, A., note 4 is not flatted in 1556 and 1588. M. 30, A., notes 5 and 6 are sm. in Fl.Ms. M. 41, T., note 2 is not flatted in 1556 and 1588. Mm. 43-44, T., note 3 of m. 43 is a dotted sb. and rest 1 of m. 44 is omitted in 1588. M. 60, T., note 3 is c in Fl.Ms. M. 78, A., note 4 is f' in Fl.Ms. M. 91, C., note 1 is a in Fl.Ms. Mm. 93-94, T., tie between these measures omitted in Fl.Ms. M. 98, A., notes 2-3 are mi. (e') tied to mi. (e') in Fl.Ms. M. 101, T., notes 1 and 2 are c', c' in Fl.Ms. Mm. 103-104, C., tie between these measures omitted in Fl.Ms. M. 112, A., note 1 is c' in Fl.Ms. M. 115, C., note 2 is d' in Fl.Ms. M. 144, C., note 3 is a' in Fl.Ms.; A., note 3 is f' in Fl.Ms.; T., note 2 is a in Fl.Ms. M. 145, T., rhythm, mi.-rest, mi., sb., sb. in Fl.Ms. M. 172, T., note 3 is a mi. in Fl.Ms.

RICERCAR [12]—M. 13, T., notes 2 and 3 are tied in Fl.Ms. M. 20, B., note 3 is not flatted in 1556. M. 23, T., last half of measure shows mi. (b-flat), sm. (b-flat), sm. (c') in Fl.Ms. Mm. 46-47, T., no tie between these measures in Fl.Ms. M. 58, A., note 3 is not flatted in 1556 and 1588. M. 60, A., note 5 is not flatted in Fl.Ms. M. 72, A., note 4 is d' in Fl.Ms. M. 80, T., notes 1 and 2 are tied together in Fl.Ms. Mm. 81-82, T., no tie between these measures in Fl.Ms. M. 87, T., note 4 is a in Fl.Ms. M. 95, B., note 2 is A in Fl.Ms. M. 96, C., notes 1 and 2 are b'-flat and c'' in Fl.Ms. M. 97, B., notes 3 and 4 are mi., mi. in Fl.Ms. M. 107, T., rhythm, mi. tied to mi., mi., mi. in Fl.Ms. M. 137, T., in Fl.Ms. the first minim's-worth reads sm. (f), fusa (g), fusa (b-flat). M. 164, A., note 4 is not flatted in 1556 and 1588. M. 187, A., notes 3 and 4 are tied in Fl.Ms. M. 191, C., note 2 has no natural sign, note 4 has a natural sign in Fl.Ms.

RICERCAR [13]—M. 14, all four voice parts in Fl.Ms. show a two-minims'-worth measure with the barline shifted from here to m. 67. M. 15, T., note 1 is b in Fl.Ms. M. 16, B., note 3 is d in Fl.Ms. M. 23, T., note 4 is f in Fl.Ms. Mm. 26-27, C., these measures are not tied in Fl.Ms. M. 29, A. and B., Fl.Ms. shows repeat signs at the end of the measure. M. 30, A., note 3 is g' in Fl.Ms. M. 31, B., Fl.Ms. shows repeat sign after note 1. M. 35, T., beats 1-2 occupied by sb.-rest in Br.Ms. Mm. 36-37, T., these measures are tied in Fl.Ms. M. 44, T., notes 1-2 tied in Fl.Ms. M. 61, B., note 4 is a in Fl.Ms. M. 67, all four voice parts in Fl.Ms. show a two-minims'-worth measure here hence correcting the misplacement of the barline from 14. M. 68, T., note 6 has no sharp in 1588. M. 71, T., note 4 is b in Fl.Ms. M. 79, T., 1588 reads sb. (e'), mi. (e'), mi. (d'). M. 85, T., Fl.Ms. reads mi. (a), 3 tied mi. (e). Mm. 95-96, A., these measures are not tied in Fl.Ms. Mm. 107-108, C., there is no tie in Fl.Ms. M. 112, A., notes 1 and 2 are f, f in Fl.Ms. M. 123, B., note 1 is f in Fl.Ms. M. 124, T., note 2 is f in Fl.Ms. M. 127, A., rhythm is mi., mi. tied to mi., mi. in Fl.Ms. M. 136, A., note 2 is b in Fl.Ms. M. 141, T., mi.-rest replaced by mi. (a) in 1588. M. 142, A., notes 3 and 4 are mi., mi. in Fl.Ms.; note 4, sources show redundant sharp sign.

RICERCAR [14]—M. 6, A., beat 4, sm. (e'), fusa (e'), fusa (f) in Fl.Ms. Mm. 14-15, A., rhythm, mi., mi. tied to mi., mi., barline, sm., sm., sm., sm., mi., mi. tied in Fl.Ms. M. 16, T., note 2 is g' in Fl.Ms. Mm. 31-32, C., note 4 of m. 31 is a' tied over barline to note 1 of m. 32, a' in Fl.Ms. M. 33, T., beat 3, sm. (b-flat), fusa (b-flat), fusa (a) in Fl.Ms. M. 35, C., Fl.Ms. reads mi. (a') tied to mi. (a') tied to mi. (a'), mi. (g'). M. 38, T., beat 3, sm. (b-flat), fusa (b-flat), fusa (c') in Fl.Ms. M. 39, C.,

note 7 is omitted in Fl.Ms. M. 47, T., beat 3 is mi. (c') tied to beat 4 mi. (c') in Fl.Ms. M. 49, A., beat 1, Fl.Ms. shows sm., fusa, fusa, all on d'; T., Fl.Ms. shows a C-clef on the fourth line. M. 50, A., note 2 is b'-flat in Fl.Ms. M. 54, C., beat 4, Fl.Ms. shows sm. (a), sm. (g). M. 64, B., beat 3, rhythm in Fl.Ms. is sm. (f), fusa (f), fusa (d). M. 65, A., note 2 is e' in Fl.Ms. M. 68, A., note 1 is b'-flat in Fl.Ms. M. 69, C., note 1 divided into two sm. (f'', f'') in Fl.Ms. M. 70, A., note 2 is b'-flat in Fl.Ms. M. 75, T., notes 2 and 3 are tied in Fl.Ms. M. 76, T., beat 2, rhythm in Fl.Ms. is sm. (a), fusa (a), fusa (b-flat). M. 85, B., from this measure to m. 111, Fl.Ms. shows rests. M. 90, T., notes 2-5, rhythm, sm., fusa, fusa, sm. in Fl.Ms. M. 103, C., beats 1-2, 1556 reads sm. (g''), sm. (f''), sm. (d''), sm. (e''); beats 3-4, Fl.Ms. rhythm is sm., sm., sm., sm. M. 104, A., note 3 is e' in Fl.Ms. M. 106, T., note 4 is f in Fl.Ms. M. 113, A., note 1 is a in Fl.Ms.

## Acknowledgments

I wish gratefully to acknowledge the permission granted by the Civico Museo Bibliografico Musicale in Bologna and the Biblioteca nazionale in Florence, owners respectively of the Malvezzi print and the manuscript, for their permission to use these sources for my edition. A debt of gratitude is owed to Mrs. Hans David, who most generously gave me her permission to consult Dr. David's transcriptions of Malvezzi's 1577 publication, and to Dr. Elinore Barber, Director of the Riemanschneider-Bach Institute at Baldwin-Wallace College, who kindly sent me a copy of those transcriptions for purposes of comparison. I have been greatly assisted in the project by a generous grant from the Research Subcommittee of Eastern New Mexico University and by the Inter-Library Loan facilities of this same institution. Three valuable assistants in copying the transcriptions were my students Mr. Floyd Sturgeon, Mr. Milford Randall Tea, and Ms. Brenda Bockstruck. And finally, I wish to express my deepest appreciation and thanks to my wife, whose patience, encouragement, and help enabled this edition to be completed.

Milton A. Swenson
Eastern New Mexico University
Portales, New Mexico

June 1977

# Notes

1. The Florentine *Camerata*, of course, is the most important academy in music history; however, it was only one of many such confraternities active throughout the Renaissance.

2. A modern edition of this anthology is in H. Colin Slim, ed., *Musica Nova* (Vol. I of *Monuments of Renaissance Music*, Edward E. Lowinsky, General Editor; Chicago: University of Chicago Press, 1964). These ricercars are analyzed in H. Colin Slim, "The Keyboard Ricercar and Fantasia in Italy, ca. 1500-1550, with Reference to Parallel Forms in European Lute Music of the Same Period" (Ph.D. diss., Harvard University, Cambridge, Massachusetts, 1960), pp. 327-33; and in Milton A. Swenson, "The Four-Part Italian Ensemble Ricercar from 1540-1619" (Ph.D. diss., Indiana University, Bloomington, Indiana, 1971), I: 23-94.

3. Jacques Buus, *Ricercari da cantare e sonare ... libro primo* (Venetia: Antonio Gardano, 1547), and Jacques Buus, *Il secondo libro di ricercari da cantare e sonare* (Venetia: Antonio Gardano, 1549). Only two of these works have been published in modern editions: "Recercar segondo" from the 1547 publication in René Lenaerts, ed., *Die Kunst der Niederländer*, Vol. 22 ("Das Musikwerk; eine Beispielsammlung zur Musikgeschichte"; Köln: A. Volk, 1962), No. 27; and "Recercar quarto" from the same 1547 edition in Wilhelm Joseph von Wasielewski, *Geschichte der Instrumental-musik im XVI. Jahrhundert mit Musikbeilagen* (Berlin: J. Guttentag, 1878), pp. 30-40. Buus' works have been studied by Gordon A. Sutherland, "The Ricercari of Jacques Buus," *The Musical Quarterly* XXXI (1945): 448-463; Hedwig Kraus, "Jacob Buus, Leben und Werke," *Tijdschrift der Vereeniging voor Nederlandsche Muziekgeschiedenis* XII (1926): 35-39; (1927): 81-96; (1928): 221-235; and Swenson, "The Four-Part Italian Ensemble Ricercar," I: 96-113.

4. Giovanni Battista Conforti, *Il Primo Libro de Ricercari* (Roma: Valero Dorico, 1558). None of these works has been published in a modern edition; however, they have been transcribed and analyzed in Swenson, "The Four-Part Italian Ensemble Ricercar," I: 185-214; II: 99-254.

5. Andrea's eight-part ricercar was published in Andrea Gabrieli and Giovanni Gabrieli, *Concerti ... Continenti Musica di Chiesa, Madrigali, & altro per voci, & stromenti Musicali ... Libro Primo et Secondo* (Venetia: Angelo Gardano, 1587). A modern edition of this piece is in Giacomo Benvenuti, ed., *Andrea e Giovanni Gabrieli e la Musica Strumentale in San Marco*, "Istituzione e Monumenti dell'Arte Musicale Italiana," 6 vols. (Milan: Ricordi, 1932), II: No. 3.

6. Andrea Gabrieli, *Madrigali et Ricercari* (Venetia: Angelo Gardano, 1589). A modern edition of all the four-part works is also by Benvenuti, *Andrea e Giovanni Gabrieli*, I. In addition, numerous modern editions have appeared of several individual pieces from this collection (namely, Ricercars III, V, and VII). Besides Benvenuti's edition, studies of Andrea Gabrieli's ensemble ricercars have been made by Gordon A. Sutherland, "Studies in the Development of the Keyboard and Ensemble Ricercare from Willaert to Frescobaldi," 2 vols. (Ph.D. diss., Harvard University, Cambridge, Massachusetts, 1942), I: 202-25; and Swenson, "The Four-Part Italian Ensemble Ricercar," I: 138-61.

7. See Swenson, "The Four-Part Italian Ensemble Ricercar," I: 159-61, for a discussion of the probable date of composition of Andrea Gabrieli's four-part ensemble ricercars.

8. Willi Apel, "The Early Development of the Organ Ricercar," *Musica Disciplina* III: 146, uses this term in reference to Andrea Gabrieli's keyboard ricercars, citing this technique as the sixteenth-century counterpart of the so-called double fugues of Bach and Handel. Also see Swenson, "The Four-Part Italian Ensemble Ricercar," I: 36-37.

9. Heinrich Glarean, *Dodekachordon* (Basle: 1547), added Modes IX to XII, with finals on a and c, to the old system of eight church modes. Andrea Gabrieli may have been one of the first composers to use these new modes for ricercars.

10. Claudio Merulo, *Il Primo Libro de Ricercari da Cantare* (Venetia: Figliuoli di Antonio Gardano, 1574); Claudio Merulo, *Ricercari da Cantare ... Libro Secondo* (Venetia: Angelo Gardano & Fratelli, 1607); Claudio Merulo, *Ricercari da Cantare ... Libro Terzo* (Venetia: Angelo Gardano & Fratelli, 1608).

11. Swenson, "The Four-Part Italian Ensemble Ricercar," I: 161-83; II: 16-98. Some general observations concerning the ricercars in Books II and III, unfortunately with missing partbooks, have been included in this analysis. According to Lawrence John Daley, "The Ricercars and Toccatas of Claudio Merulo" (Master's thesis, Graduate College, University of Illinois, 1967), p. 50, Book II (1607) and Book III (1608) were "posthumous reprints of this collection from 1574." This is an erroneous statement, since every one of Merulo's sixty ensemble ricercars is a new and different piece. Daley's thesis, which presumes to include a detailed discussion and analysis of Merulo's ensemble ricercars, is based upon completely false assumptions and is greatly lacking in accuracy. For a more complete discussion of this, see Swenson, "The Four-Part Italian Ensemble Ricercar," I: 16-18.

12. According to Apel, *Geschichte der Orgel- und Klaviermusik bis 1700* (Kassel: Bärenreiter-Verlag, 1967), pp. 177-78, Merulo used this same technique in his Ricercar II from the keyboard publication of 1567, which, as Apel states, may be called an "Umkehrungsfuge."

13. Bianca Becherini, "Malvezzi, Cristoforo," *MGG*, VIII: col. 1554. Riccardo Gandolfi, *Appunti di Storia Musicale: Cristofano Malvezzi, Emilio de' Cavalieri* (Firenze: Uffizio della Rassegna Nazionale, 1893), pp. 5-6, cites June 28 as the date Malvezzi was registered for baptism, with the likelihood that he was born the day before, June 27th; as Gandolfi states: "All' Archivio Parrocchiale di S. Frediano in Lucca, trovasi citato al foglio 45 del libro sesto dei battezzati: 'a di 28 giugno 1547 Cristofano di Nicolajo Malvezzi organista,' ciò che induce a ritenere che questo infante avesse visto la luce il giorno innanzi, cioè il 27 giugno."

14. Becherini, "Malvezzi."

15. H. Colin Slim, "The Keyboard Ricercar and Fantasia in Italy," p. 136, citing from "Documenten betreffende de Muziekkapel aan Hof van Ferrara," *Bulletin de l'Institut Historique Belge de Rome* XX (1939): 212. Also lending credence to Cristofano's association with Brumel is the fact, cited by

Gandolfi, *Appunti,* p. 6, that Nicolao Malvezzi's successor in 1557 as organist at San Martini was "the notable Jacopo Corsini, student in Ferrara of the famous Flemish [Jaches] Brumel"; quoting from Gandolfi: " ... col successore di lui [Nicolao Malvezzi], l'insigne Iacopo Corsini, alunno in Ferrara del famoso fiammingo Brumel."

16. Becherini, "Malvezzi."

17. Gandolfi, *Appunti,* to quote: "Da appunti gentilmente favoritimi dal Reverendo Canonico Lagi di S. Lorenzo resulta che il Malvezzi nel 1572 preso possesso di un canonicato in quella Basilica, già tenuto da un tal Donato Valdambrini morto nel 1571, e che al Malvezzi successe come canonico nel 1599 certo Francesco Petrelli." Becherini, "Malvezzi," without citing her source, states that Malvezzi had held this post since 1562: "Seit 1562 Domherr an San Lorenzo. ... " Robert Eitner, *Biographisch-Bibliographisches Quellen-Lexikon der Musiker und Musikgelehrten der Christlichen Zeitrechnung bis zur Mitte des 19. Jahrhunderts,* photolithographed edition, 11 vols. (New York: Musurgia, 1947), VI: 289, cites "21. April 1571" as the date Malvezzi became canon.

18. According to Gandolfi, *Appunti,* two others were appointed to this position in the time between Corteccia and Malvezzi, namely: Piero Manenti in 1571 after Corteccia's death and Giovanni del Cartolaro at the time Manenti became organist at S. Maria del Fiore, to quote: " ... chè lo vediamo indi nominato maestro della Cappello Granducale, ufficio al quale erano già stati successivamente elevati Francesco Corteccia nel 1539 e nel 1571 Piero Manenti, sostituito da Giovanni del Cartolaro quando il Manenti passò organist di S. Maria del Fiore."

19. A description of these intermezzi may be found in Gandolfi, *Appunti,* pp. 4-5, and Gustave Reese, *Music in the Renaissance* (New York: W. W. Norton, 1954), pp. 566-70.

20. Donald P. Walker, "Bardi, Giovanni, Conte di Vernio," *MGG,* I: col. 1256; the citation reads as follows: "Zu diesem zwanglosen Gelehrtenkreis [the 'Camerato Fiorentina'] gehörten mit Sicherheit Galilei, Caccini, Peri, Pietro Strozzi, wahrscheinlich auch Cavalieri (nach 1584), Mei, Rinuccini, Corsi, Malvezzi." Furthermore, the fact that Malvezzi dedicated his ricercar publication to Count Bardi indicates that this wealthy nobleman was Malvezzi's patron as early as 1577.

21. A modern edition of music composed and performed for these wedding festivities is by Donald P. Walker, ed., *Musique des intermèdes de "La Pellegrina": Malvezzi, Marenzio, Caccini, Bardi, Peri, Cavalieri,* Vol. I of "Les Fêtes du mariage de Ferdinand de Médicis et de Christine de Lorraine, Florence 1589" (Paris: Centre National de la Recherche Scientifique, 1963).

22. One madrigal in Felice Anerio, *Le Gioie* (Venedig: R. Amadino, 1589); one in *Vittoria amorosa* (Venedig: G. Vincenti, 1596); one in *Ghirlanda* (Löwen: Phalèse, 1601); and two in Orfeo Vecchi, *Scelta de Madrigali à quinta voci* (Mailand: Tini & Lomazzo, 1604).

23. Located in Florence, Biblioteca Nazionale Centrale, Ms. Magliabecchi 66, XIX, fols. 83-87. Cited by William V. Porter, "Peri and Corsi's *Dafne:* Some New Discoveries and Observations," *JAMS* XVIII (1965): 192.

24. Bernhard Schmiden, *Tabulatur Buch von Allerhand ausserlesenen, Schönen, Lieblichen Praeludijs, Toccaten, Motteten, Canzonetten, Madrigalien unnd Fugen von 4. 5. und 6. Stimmen ...* (Strassburg: Lazari Zetzners, 1607). Although Becherini, "Malvezzi," does not make note of this piece by Malvezzi, it

is cited by Claudio Sartori, *Bibliografia della Musica Strumentale Italiana Stampata in Italia Fino al 1700* (Firenze: Leo S. Olschki, 1952), p. 148, who lists the complete contents of Schmid's organ tablature; and Apel, *Geschichte der Orgel- und Klaviermusik bis 1700,* pp. 196-97, who describes it as follows: "Bei Bernhard Schmid d. J. wird dann Fuge mit Canzone identifiziert. Sein *Tabulatur-Buch* von 1607 enhält eine Gruppe von Stücken mit der Überschrift: 'Fugen (oder wie es die Italiener nennen) *Canzoni alla Francese.*' Hier werden Instrumentalcanzonen von Brignoli, [Christoffano] Malvezio, Maschera, Gabrieli und andern Italienern intabuliert und als *Fuga prima, Fuga secunda* usw. bezeichnet." A manuscript transcription of this piece is in Alfred Einstein, "A Collection of Instrumental Music of the Sixteenth-Eighteenth Centuries" (9 vols.; unpublished manuscript transcriptions, available on microfilm from the Smith College Archives, Northampton, Mass.), VIII: No. 66; a reprint of Malvezzi's intabulated Fuga may be found in August F. Ritter, *Zur Geschichte des Orgelspiels* (Leipzig: 1884), vol. II, "Musikalische Beispiele," No. 9.

25. Federico Ghisi, "Peri, Jacopo," *MGG,* X: col. 1064.

26. Federico Ghisi, "Peri," X: cols. 1064-66. This biography includes a cut showing "Jacopo Peri ('Zazzerino') als Arion im 5. Intermedium anlässlich der Hochzeit Ferdinandos I. Medici, 1589."

27. Letter from Emilio de' Cavalieri in Rome to Marcello Accolti, secretary to the grand duke in Florence; preserved in Florence, *Archivio di stato, Archivio mediceo del principato,* Filza 3622, fol. 186; cited by Claude V. Palisca, "Musical Asides in the Diplomatic Correspondence of Emilio de' Cavalieri," *MQ* XLIX (1963): 353.

28. The letter was written by Pietro de' Bardi, son of the first patron of the Florentine *Camerata,* to Giovan Battista Doni. Translated by Oliver Strunk, *Source Readings in Music History: The Baroque Era* (New York: W. W. Norton & Company, 1965), p. 4.

29. Ghisi, "Peri." The Duchess of Mantua was Eleanore de' Medici, eldest daughter of Grand Duke Francesco de' Medici and Joanna of Austria. Eleanore was married to Vincenzo Gonzaga, Duke of Mantua, in 1583.

30. Oscar G. Sonneck, " 'Dafne,' the First Opera. A Chronological Study," *Sammelbände der Internationalen Musikgesellschaft* XV (1913-1914): 104; cited in Porter, "Peri and Corsi's *Dafne,*" p. 171. Porter, pp. 170-96, also discusses some recent additional discoveries of pieces from this first opera.

31. This opera was presented in Mantua to celebrate the wedding of Francisco Gonzaga, son of Eleanore de' Medici and Vincenzo Gonzaga (cf. above, no. 29), to Margherita of Savoy. Unfortunately, the only music from this opera to have survived is Monteverdi's well-known aria "Lamento d'Arianna." This wedding celebration also witnessed the performance of another opera, namely Marco da Gagliano's *Dafne,* which also was based on Rinuccini's libretto.

32. Ghisi, "Peri," col. 1066.

33. Giacomo Benvenuti, ed., *Andrea e Giovanni Gabrieli,* I: xliii-xliv.

34. Joel Newman, "A Gentleman's Lute Book: The Tablature of Gabriello Fallamero," *Current Musicology* II (Fall 1965): 179. Hans Klotz, "Annibale Pado(v)ano," *MGG,* I: col. 491, states that Padovano did not leave Venice until 1566.

35. There is disagreement among musicologists as to which one of the two organs was Padovano's appointment.

According to Benvenuti, *Andrea e Giovanni Gabrieli*, p. xxxix, he was assigned to the second organ, while both Klotz, "Annibale Pado(v)ano," col. 491, and Giacomo del Valle de Paz, *Annibale Padovano nella Storia della Musica del Cinquecento* (Turin: Bocca, 1933), state that he was appointed to the first organ.

36. André Pirro, *L'Art des Organistes, Part II, Encyclopédie de la Musique*, ed. Alexandre Lavignac, 11 vols. (Paris: 1913-1939), II: 1191; cited by Pierront and Hennebains, eds., *Annibale Padovano Ricercari* (Paris: Editions de l'oiseau lyre, Louis B. M. Dyer, 1934), p. 8.

37. Félix-Alexandre Guilmant and André Pirro, eds., *Archives des Maîtres de l'Orgue des XVIe, XVIIe, et XVIIIe Siècles*, 10 vols. (Paris: Durand, 1898-1914), X:vii, as cited in Pierront and Hennebains, *Annibale Padovano Ricercari*, p. 8.

38. Hellmut Federhofer, "Musik am Grazer Habsburgerhof der Erzherzöge Karl II. und Ferdinand (1564-1619)," *Oesterreichische Musikzeitschrift* XXV (October 1970): 588.

39. Federhofer, "Musik am Grazer Habsburgerhof," pp. 588-89.

40. Federhofer, "Musik am Grazer Habsburgerhof," p. 589.

41. Federhofer, "Musik am Grazer Habsburgerhof," p. 590.

42. According to Federhofer, "Musik am Grazer Habsburgerhof," pp. 588-89, Johannes de Cleve may have been released from his position at the Catholic Court of Graz because of his sympathies towards the Lutheran movement.

43. Federhofer, "Musik am Grazer Habsburgerhof," p. 590.

44. Federhofer, "Musik am Grazer Habsburgerhof," p. 589, " . . . es ist mir gar leit vmb sein Kunst, vmb in; iezt wird mein schlagen shon ein loch haben."

45. Translated in Oliver Strunk, *Source Readings in Music History: The Renaissance* (New York: W. W. Norton, 1965), p. 130.

46. *Toccate et Ricercari di'organo del Escellentissimo Annibali Padoano, gia organista della Serenissima Signoria di Venetia: Nouamenta Stampate, e date in luce* (In Venetia: Angelo Gardano, 1604). This keyboard publication, in *partitura* or open score notation, contains eight toccatas and two ricercars. Only the first three toccatas and the two ricercars are by Padovano; authorship of the last five toccatas is unknown. A modern edition of the two ricercars in this source is in Luigi Torchi, ed., *Composizioni per Organo o Cembalo, Secolo XVI, XVII, XVIII, L'Arte Musicale in Italia* (Milano: G. Ricordi, 1897-1908), III: 79-90; and the second of these two ricercars is published in Gino Tagliapietra, ed., *Antologia di Musica Antica e Moderna per Pianoforte*, 14 vols. (Milano: G. Ricordi, 1931-32), I: 94 ff.

47. Annibale Podoana [*sic*] and Andrea Gabrieli, *Dialoghi Musicali de Diversi Eccellentissimi Autori . . . con Due Battaglie a Otto Voci* (Venetia: Angelo Gardano, 1590). A reprint appeared in 1592. A modern edition of Padovano's piece is in Benvenuti, ed., *Andrea e Giovanni Gabrieli*, I: No. 12.

48. Federhofer, "Musik am Grazer Habsburgerhof," p. 590.

49. I am indebted to Gordon Sutherland, "Studies in the Development of the Keyboard and Ensemble Ricercare from Willaert to Frescobaldi," 2 vols. (Ph.D. diss., Harvard University, 1942) I: 165-73, and to Pierront and Hennebains, *Annibale Padovano Ricercari* for part of the analysis of Padovano's ricercars.

50. Padovano also employs this technique, but not in the five pieces represented in the present edition. As is cited in Swenson, "The Four-Part Italian Ensemble Ricercar," I: 122, rhythmic transformation occurs particularly in two of the works: "Ricercar del Settimo Tono," where the rhythmic values of both theme A (mm. 1-118) and theme C (mm. 157-189) are constantly varied, and "Ricercar del Ottavo Tono," theme B. These are Ricercars II and VI respectively according to Padovano's 1556 publication and the Pierront and Hennebains edition. The earliest example of this technique of constant rhythmic variation of the theme is found in Giuliano Tiburtino's twelve monothematic ricercars which were published in *Fantasie, Recherchari a tre voci* (Venice: Scotus, 1549); see Imogene Horsley, "The Monothematic Ricercari of Giuliano Tiburtino," abstract of a paper read at a meeting of the Midwest Chapter AMS in East Lansing, Michigan on May 18, 1957, *JAMS* IX (Fall 1956): 242-44.

51. From the *hexachordum naturale* to the *hexachordum durum*. See Willi Apel, *Harvard Dictionary of Music*, 2nd ed. (Cambridge: The Belknap Press of Harvard University Press, 1969), pp. 383-84.

52. A key signature of one flat usually indicates a transposed mode, but not always. Pietro Aron, *Trattato della Natura e Cognizione di Tutti gli Toni di Canto Figurato* (Venice: 1525), chap. vi; translated in Strunk, *Source Readings in Music History* (New York: W. W. Norton, 1950), pp. 215-16, points out that Modes V and VI, with a final on f, almost always have a b-flat key signature. This is, of course, how the "F-major" tonality got its start. There is no explanation in Aron's treatise for the tonality of one of Padovano's ricercars (not contained in the present edition). The last piece in his 1556 publication, "Ricercar del Sesto Tono," ends with a final cadence on c, but lacks the b-flat key signature.

53. Pierront and Hennebains, eds., *Annibale Padovano Ricercari*, p. 18, discusses Padovano's use of chant melodies in his ricercars. Also compare this theme with the *Kyrie* melody in *Liber Usualis*, Benedictines of Solesmes, eds. (Tournai: Desclée & cie, 1956), p. 25.

54. Pierront and Hennebains, eds., *Annibale Padovano Ricercari*, p. 18.

55. Compare *Liber Usualis*, p. 957.

56. *Liber Usualis*, p. 113. Pierront and Hennebains designate this melody as Themes IIIa and IIIb.

57. *Liber Usualis*, pp. 957 and 115 respectively. Pierront and Hennebains identify these two melodies as Theme I (*Qui pacem ponit*) and Theme IV (Fifth Psalm Tone).

58. Pierront and Hennebains, eds., *Annibale Padovano Ricercari*, p. 19. This canzona appeared in Maschera's *Libro Primo de Canzoni da Sonare a quattro voci* (In Brescia: Appresso Vincenzo Sabio, M. D. LXXXIIII), No. 18. Maschera may have appropriated this theme from Padovano rather than the other way around.

59. Sutherland, "Keyboard and Ensemble Ricercare," I: 166.

60. Ricercar del Settimo Tono, which is No. II in the 1556 publication, has an opening exposition extending to the length of twenty-three measures; this piece has a codetta which features a two-part canon.

61. I cannot agree with Sutherland, "Keyboard and Ensemble Ricercare," I: 167, when he states that Annibale uses more "scholastic counterpoint" than any composer before Andrea Gabrieli, nor with his statement that "in most of Annibale's ricercari he appears to employ contrapuntal artifice for its own sake." In the first place, Jacques Buus, Giulio

Segni, and Guilielmo Colin all used these contrapuntal devices quite frequently. (See Swenson, "The Four-Part Italian Ensemble Ricercar," I: 100-101, 107, 53, 78.) Secondly, in order to understand the logic of Padovano's "contrapuntal artifice for its own sake" one must recognize that many of his themes were taken from Gregorian chant, a fact which is nowhere mentioned in Sutherland's study even though Pierront and Hennebains before him had discussed at length this feature of Padovano's themes.

62. Sutherland, "Keyboard and Ensemble Ricercare," I: 170.

63. Sutherland, "Keyboard and Ensemble Ricercare," I: 168.

64. Sutherland, "Keyboard and Ensemble Ricercare," I: 168.

65. See note 52 above.

66. The somewhat out-of-date edition of these works by N. Pierront and J. P. Hennebains, eds., *Annibale Padovano Ricercari*, makes no notice of the double clef signs and key signature even though the two editors must have come across them when transcribing the music from the sixteenth-century sources. Two other writers on Padovano's ricercars: Gordon Sutherland, "Keyboard and Ensemble Ricercare," I: 162-73; and Richard M. Murphy, "Fantasia and Ricercare in the Sixteenth Century" (Ph.D. diss., Yale University, 1954), pp. 188-89, seem to have been totally ignorant of these peculiarities. The first discussion of them is in Swenson, "The Four-Part Italian Ensemble Ricercar," I: 132-37.

67. From a study of late Renaissance theoretical sources Arthur Mendel, "Pitch in the Sixteenth and Early Seventeenth Century," *MQ* XXXIV (1948): 336-38, and others have recognized two sets of clefs in common usage and defined by contemporary theorists. The first was called *chiavi naturali,* having a C-clef on line 1 in the Cantus, a C-clef on line 3 in the Altus, a C-clef on line 4 in the Tenor, and an F-clef on line 4 in the Bass. The *low chiavette,* which was the other set, had a C-clef on line 2 in the Cantus, a C-clef on line 4 in the Altus, an F-clef on line 3 in the Tenor, and an F-clef on line 5 in the Bass.

68. See Swenson, "The Four-Part Italian Ensemble Ricercar," I: 133-36, for a more detailed analysis of this problem and its solution.

69. Apel, *Orgel-und Klaviermusik,* p. 176. The procedure by which Padovano arrives at the key of "D major" is worthy of note. Many sixteenth-century compositions written in Mode VI, with their final on f, have a key signature of b-flat. These pieces therefore represent early examples of the use of the "F-major" key. In order to arrive at his new "D-major" tonality Padovano simply had to transpose this "major" Mode VI down a minor third (*alla terza*), using a key signature of two sharps. This procedure is not unlike that used in his earlier ensemble work, Ricercar [15].

70. The *Scuoli grandi* and the part they played in Renaissance art, literature, and music is discussed by Denis Arnold, "Music at a Venetian Confraternity in the Renaissance," *Acta Musicologia* XXXVII (1965): 62-72, and Denis Arnold, "Music at the Scuola di San Rocco," *Music and Letters* XL (1959): 229-41.

71. Since the natural sign had not yet come to be generally used in sixteenth-century notation, both the sharp and the flat signs were used for this purpose: the sharp sign to raise a pitch which had previously been flatted (i.e., in the key signature), and the flat sign to lower a pitch which had previously been sharped.

72. For an explanation of the hexachordal system, see Apel, *Harvard Dictionary of Music,* rev. ed., pp. 383-85; also Martin Ruhnke, "Hexachord," *MGG,* VI: cols. 349-58.

73. Until recently this library was named the Biblioteca Comunale annessa al Conservatorio Musicale G. B. Martini.

74. Bianca Becherini, *Catalogo dei Manoscritti Musicali della Biblioteca Nazionale di Firenze* (Kassel: Bärenreiter, 1959).

75. This manuscript was formerly designated as Magliabecchi, Cl. XIX, 107.

76. Hans David had been working on a modern edition of Malvezzi's ricercars; this edition was scheduled to be published in the *Monuments of Renaissance Music* series (Edward E. Lowinsky, General Editor; Chicago: University of Chicago Press, 1964-). Due to Dr. David's death in 1967, the edition was never completed. This made it necessary for me to reconstruct and transcribe these ricercars for my doctoral dissertation.

77. Edward E. Lowinsky, "Early Scores in Manuscript," *JAMS* XIII (1960): 136-73, includes as one of his matters of discussion the problem of dating manuscript scores by their handwriting. He states (pp. 134-35) that: "Sixteenth-century writing in Italy is known for its concern with the form of each individual letter, . . . 17th-century writing for its greater speed, the stronger inclination toward the right, the more thorough joining of letters, the greater impetus and energy of lines, curves, and loops, and the resulting decrease in attention given to the shape of the single letters. . . . Toward the end of the 16th and the first years of the 17th centuries we find various stages of transition . . . marked by slowly increasing speed and joining of letters with a corresponding gradual loss of interest in the shape of a single letter." Further (n. 24), " . . . the graphological evidence of a change in the style of writing from Renaissance to Baroque moves in the same direction: from repose to motion." A comparison of the last eight pages with the main part of the manuscript clearly illustrates just this change of writing style: from one of repose, with a degree of concern for the form of each note, to one of motion, with greater speed, the note stems being curved and inclined toward the right.

78. Neither Ghisi, "Peri," nor any of Peri's other biographers have attributed this ricercar to him. About eleven years ago, however, Hans David discovered Jacopo Peri's authorship of this piece, but had not been able to publish this finding before his death in 1967. I first became aware of Dr. David's prior discovery in 1971 thanks to the generous assistance of his widow, and Dr. Elinore Barber, Director of the Riemanschneider-Bach Institute, Baldwin-Wallace College, who is collecting and editing Dr. David's unpublished material. Mrs. David kindly informed me of the existence of an unpublished brief essay concerning Jacopo Peri written by her late husband in 1967. This essay, most appropriately entitled "Little Long Hair," discusses his discovery of this previously unknown work by Peri. The essay is soon to be published in a collection of *Baroque and Renaissance Essays* by Hans T. David, edited by Elinore Barber.

79. According to Pierront and Hennebains, eds., *Annibale Padovano Ricercari,* p. 17, this is not the case, for they state that in the two posthumous editions of Padovano's ricercars added colorations are abundantly seen ("Nous ajouterons la remarque suivante: l'édition princeps 1556 ne comparte pas de coloratures, contrairement aux deux posterieures [1588 and 1604] qui en sont abandamment pourvues . . . "). While this statement indeed holds true for the two ricercars in the 1604 keyboard publication, I have made a careful comparison of the 1588 reprint with the 1556 edition and found only

a few minor instances where the music of the two editions does not correspond exactly.

80. A reproduction of the dedication appears in Edward E. Lowinsky, "Early Scores in Manuscript," Plate 6 (between pp. 148 and 149). Lowinsky, pp. 134-35, also describes the Brussels manuscript and deduces from the style of the handwriting in the dedication that it was done in the seventeenth century.

81. Sperindio Bertoldo, *Tocate Ricercari et Canzoni Francese intavolate per sonar d'organo.* Nuovamente Stampati (In Venetia: Appresso Giacomo Vicenti, M. D. XCI). No. 4 = Ricercar IV of the 1556 ed., No. 5 = Ricercar I of the 1556 ed. Cited by Howard Mayer Brown, *Instrumental Music Printed before 1600: A Bibliography* (Cambridge: Harvard University Press, 1965), pp. 173-74, 368. Brown, p. 368, incorrectly lists Padovano's Ricercar V as Ricercar I. Bertoldo's source is printed in keyboard score. A modern edition of these two intabulated ricercars may be found in Luigi Torchi, ed., *Composizioni per Organo*, pp. 55 and 58. Torchi incorrectly ascribes these pieces to Bertoldo Sperindio [*sic*] instead of to Annibale Padovano. Further on these works, see Willi Apel, *Geschichte der Orgel- und Klaviermusik bis 1700*, pp. 176-77.

82. Vincenzo Galilei, *Fronimo Dialogo ... sopra l'Arte del Bene Intavolare, et Rettamente Sonare la Musica* (In Vineggia: Appresso l'Herede di Girolamo Scotto, M. D. LXXXIIII), No. 2; cited by Brown, *Instrumental Music Printed before 1600*, p. 173.

83. Gabriel Fallamero, *Il Primo Libro de Intavolatura da Liuto* (Vinegia: l'Herede di Girolamo Scotto, 1584), Nos. 42 and 41 respectively. Concordances cited from Brown, *Instrumental Music Printed before 1600*, p. 174.

84. N. Pierront and J. P. Hennebains, ed., *Annibale Padovano Ricercari.*

Plate I. Cristofano Malvezzi, *Il Primo Libro de Ricercari* (1577):
title page and first page of Altus of No. 1, "Ricercar del Terzo Tuono."
(Courtesy, Civico Museo Bibliografico Musicale, Bologna)

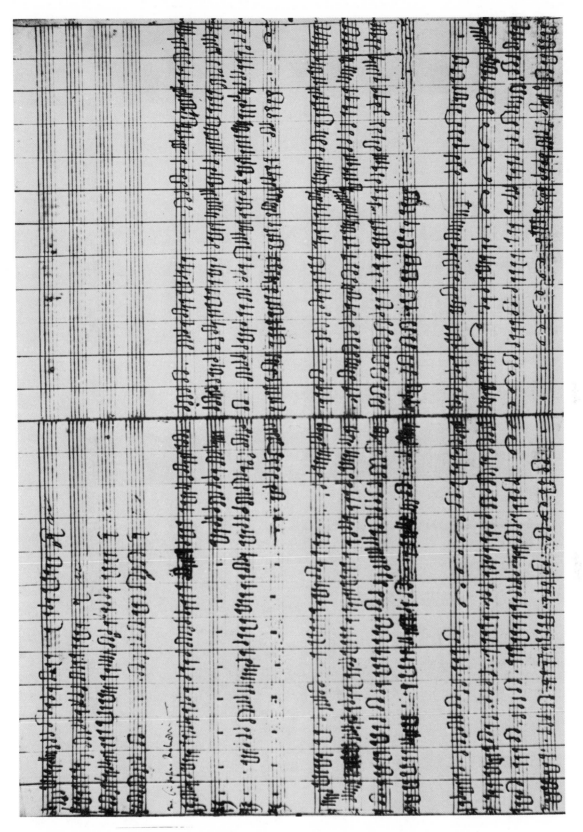

Plate II. Florence, Ms. Mus. II.I.295 (formerly Magliabecchi, Cl. XIX. 107), folios 38ᵛ-39: second system of folio 38ᵛ shows beginning of Malvezzi's "Ricercar del Terzo Tuono" (No. 1). (Courtesy, Biblioteca nazionale, Florence)

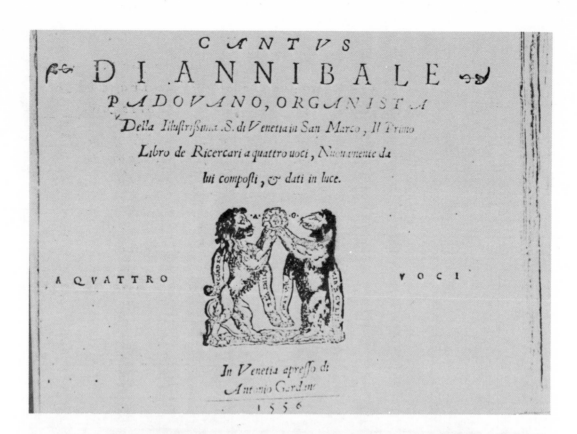

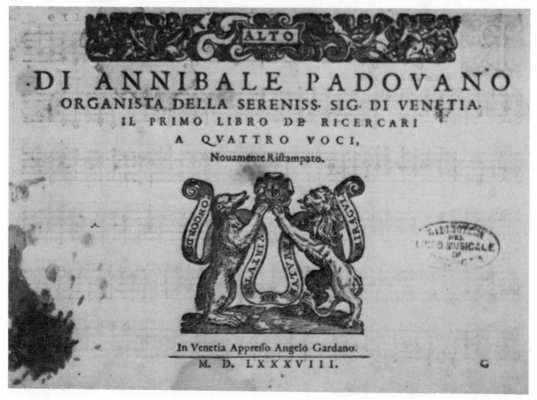

Plate III. Title pages of Annibale Padovano's *Il Primo Libro de Ricercari a quattro voci,* 1556 (Cantus part), and the Reprint, dated 1588 (Alto part). (Courtesy, Royal College of Music Library, London; Civico Museo Bibliografico Musicale, Bologna)

# ENSEMBLE RICERCARS

# [1.] Ricercar del Terzo Tuono

Cristofano Malvezzi

2

# [2.] Ricercar del Secondo Tuono

Cristofano Malvezzi

6

8

## [3.] Ricercar del Secondo Tuono

Cristofano Malvezzi

## [4.] Ricercar del Primo Tuono

Cristofano Malvezzi

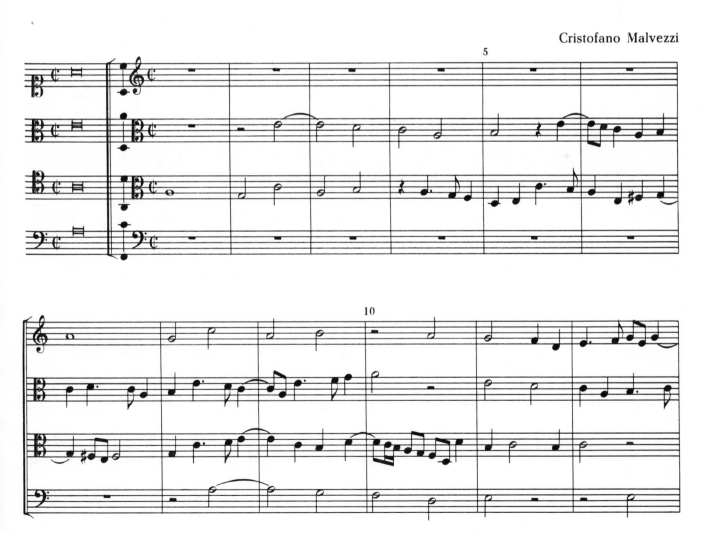

14

## [5.] Ricercar del Ottavo Tuono

Cristofano Malvezzi

# [6.] Ricercar senza unisoni del Duodecimo Tuono

Cristofano Malvezzi

24

26

# [7.] Ricercar del Settimo Tuono

Cristofano Malvezzi

# [8.] Ricercar del Undecimo Tuono

Cristofano Malvezzi

## [9.] Ricercar del Primo Tuono Del Zazzerino

[Jacopo Peri]

# [10.] Ricercar del Terzo Tuono

Cristofano Malvezzi

# [11.] Ricercar del Primo Tono

Annibale Padovano

# [12.] Ricercar del Secondo Tono

Annibale Padovano

[sic.]

# [13.] Ricercar del Terzo Tono

Annibale Padovano

# [14.] Ricercar del Quinto Tono

Annibale Padovano

## [15.] Ricercar del Primo Tono
[Transposed Version]

Annibale Padovano